ENDORSEMENTS

JIMMY DEYOUNG

PRESIDENT & FOUNDER, PROPHECY TODAY

"David James has done an excellent job in this book, a review of the book, *The Harbinger*, being very careful not to bring personality into focus but instead to take a crucial look at the biblical aspects of the book. Having read the book a number of times, David studied the hermeneutic used in the book to examine the use of a single passage of scripture taken out of context to understand what the author had done to develop a fictional book while at the same time telling the reader that everything in the book was real.

"I believe that David did the research required to give a fair look at Jonathan Cahn's work and, at the same time, apply the age-old truths of Bible interpretation to help any potential reader of *The Harbinger* to be aware of the problems in this work. I know that David spent much time in prayer and consultation before he approached the writing of his review, and his only desire is to hold up the truth that we don't get doctrine, or our understanding of Bible prophecy, from a fictional novel but from the Word of God, the Bible."

BRANNON HOWSE

PRESIDENT & FOUNDER, WORLDVIEW WEEKEND

"All across America hundreds of thousands of people have purchased Jonathan Cahn's book, *The Harbinger*. By far, the majority have given it rave reviews as well as promoted it, defended it, and recommended it to everyone they know. Unfortunately, this represents a pervasive lack of biblical knowledge and discernment in the church and is why many of us have written and broadcast our deep concerns about the book. I believe David James has used true discernment, extensive research, and biblical hermeneutics to reveal the dangerous message of *The Harbinger*. James's research also defends the authority of Scripture against the increasing trend of experience, extra-biblical revelation, and mysticism."

[continued next page]

PAUL BARRECA

Teaching Pastor, Faith Bible Church
Vineland, New Jersey

"Whether or not you've read *The Harbinger*, you must read David James's thorough and thoughtful response in *The Harbinger: Fact or Fiction?* The popularity of Cahn's book has many Christians wondering if the Bible contains a secret message for America enveloped in the details of the 9/11 terrorist attacks. I recognized a dangerous hermeneutic at work in Jonathan Cahn's fast-paced novel but was daunted by the challenge of providing a response for my congregation. David James provides such a response. This book gives the reader a detailed, point-by-point analysis challenging Cahn's barrage of data and 'connect the dot' attempts. David James does this with clear biblical methodology while avoiding personal attacks against Cahn. This book is an example of the way that Christian dialogue should be conducted."

ROY B. ZUCK

Senior Professor Emeritus of Bible Exposition
Editor, *Bibliotheca Sacra*
Dallas Theological Seminary

"Jonathan Cahn's book *The Harbinger* has been a bestseller for many months. A messianic Jew, Cahn is the senior pastor of the Jerusalem/Beth Israel Worship Center in Wayne, New Jersey. *The Harbinger* presents the view that Isaiah 9:10-11 refers to the United States, and in particular to the catastrophe of 9/11 and the States' subsequent economic problems. James masterfully demolishes Cahn's efforts to relate this passage to the States, pointing up numerous hermeneutical and interpretive fallacies in Cahn's approach. Anyone interested in *The Harbinger* needs to note the numerous errors in Cahn's thinking, as presented in James's excellent analysis."

GARY E. GILLEY

Senior Pastor, Southern View Chapel, Springfield, Illinois
Director, Think on These Things Ministries

"Jonathan Cahn's *The Harbinger* is a warning to America that God's judgment is imminent unless the country repents and turns to the Lord, and that very soon. If the book is read merely as a novel warning our country to wake up spiritually, it has value, but the author makes immediately clear that 'what is contained within the story is real' (p. 7). In other words, Cahn believes that God pronounced exacting judgment on America, and that judgment is found in Scripture, specifically Isaiah 9:10-11.

[continued next page]

"Cahn determines that this text in Isaiah contains a mysterious prophecy directed not to ancient Israel but to modern America. At this point the author massages Scripture, American history, and current events in an attempt to prove that God's judgment on the United States has been hiding in these verses but has now been unlocked by the careful investigation of Cahn. Once someone decides they can cherry-pick verses at will, change the meaning of these texts to fit one's theories, and use random hermeneutical methods, anything can be 'proven.' However, very few people will recognize what Cahn has done, and fewer still will do the hard work of investigating his interpretations.

"Here is where David James has greatly benefitted the body of Christ. He has carefully, graciously and thoroughly analyzed the claims found in *The Harbinger* and found many of them lacking biblical support and historical accuracy. James has written this book not merely to expose error but to keep God's people from being led astray by false teachings and improper hermeneutical approaches to Scripture. I believe he has accomplished these goals in *The Harbinger: Fact or Fiction?*"

TOMMY ICE

EXECUTIVE DIRECTOR, PRE-TRIB RESEARCH CENTER
PASTOR/TEACHER AND CHURCH PLANTER,
COMMUNITY BIBLE CHURCH, OMAHA, NEBRASKA

"Just because something is popular within today's evangelical community does not mean that it is biblical. *The Harbinger* is a popular book for many within evangelicalism that claims to provide a message from God, but it is not built upon a true biblical foundation. Dave James provides a fair biblical analysis for anyone wanting scrutiny of *The Harbinger*. I commend James's book, *The Harbinger: Fact or Fiction?*, for those seeking the truth rather than popularity."

LARRY DEBRUYN

GUARDING HIS FLOCK MINISTRIES

"In a fair and balanced way, Dave James exposes the eccentric biblical interpretations upon which *The Harbinger* is premised. He demonstrates biblical and theological inaccuracies contained in the story created by Jonathan Cahn, one which the author claims to be partially real. James connects the dots between multiple biblical, historical, and factual problems, which gives the reader the sense that *The Harbinger* has undertones of Anglo-Israelism and Christian Dominionism. Though perhaps not intended by the author, these concepts form an underlying philosophical framework upon which the theoretical 'secret' of America's future appears to be based. For readers possessing a heart to discern truth from error, *The Harbinger: Fact or Fiction?* frames fundamental issues related to an accurate understanding of Bible prophecy in our modern world. Highly recommended."

[continued next page]

LARRY J. WATERS

ASSOCIATE PROFESSOR OF BIBLE EXPOSITION

DALLAS THEOLOGICAL SEMINARY

"One of the most asked questions in biblical prophecy today is, 'Where does the United States fit into eschatology?' Jonathan Cahn's *The Harbinger* tries to answer that question—however, he attempts to do so with many unfounded hermeneutical 'jumps' that cannot be sustained. Dave James goes to great lengths to debunk Cahn's theories and offers a balanced look at end-time prophecy and the USA. Where Scripture is silent, it is best not to impose one's own presumptions on the text. For those interested in this subject, James offers extensive objections to Cahn's presumptions."

THE

HARBINGER

FACT OR FICTION?

DAVID JAMES

The **Berean Call**

BEND • OREGON

CONTENTS

FOREWORD

For the time will come

For the time will come
when they will not endure sound doctrine...

II Timothy 4:3

ONE OF THE MOST grievous experiences in my 35 years of ministry has been the ongoing observation of evangelicals being weaned off the Word of God. What has contributed to that tragic development for the last three decades is a myriad of programs, practices, methods, and books that have, to one degree or another, displaced the authority and sufficiency of the Scriptures. In my association with Dave Hunt over that period of time, we have addressed most of those trends and teachings in books such as *The Seduction of Christianity*, and for the last twenty years have documented our concerns in *The Berean Call* newsletters.

Although the church historically has always had to deal with false teachings and practices, the exponential rate of their influence in our day is the result of what has been referred to as the Church Growth Movement and its dependence upon marketing to bring the lost into the church. The outcome of this very popular movement was disastrous for Bible-believing churches that succumbed to a marketing mentality and process. Bible teaching was relegated to Wednesday evening so as not to put off the lost who showed up on Sunday. More often than not, such evening "Bible studies" featured the popular Christian books of the day rather than the inspired Books of God's Word. In accordance with the key principle of marketing, the lost as well as believers who were drawn to the church (because of the attractive new programs) were viewed as consumers who were not to be offended because that might prevent them from coming back. After all, customer relationship rules in the "seeker-sensitive, seeker-friendly" approach to church growth.

This development, perhaps more that any other in our day, created a drift and then a swift current, pulling evangelicals away from the Scriptures. Again, the results were and continue to be disastrous. How so? The ongoing process of weaning those who profess to be Bible-believing Christians away from God's Word has left them terribly vulnerable to false doctrine. To the degree that a believer has drifted from Scripture, to that degree he or she has lost the ability to discern God's truth from "a way that seems right to a man" and to that degree will be subject to spiritual deception (Proverbs 14:12, 16:25).

Jesus characterized the days prior to His return by telling His disciples: "Take heed that no man deceive you" (Matthew 24:4), and followed that by warning that the deceptions of the last days would be so overwhelming that "if possible, they shall deceive the very elect" (Matthew 24:24). What is the antidote for believers? It's quite simple. They must be disciplined in their reading and living out the instructions of God's Word. They must have a love for the Truth. They must become like the Bereans of Acts 17:10-11, who were commended for searching the Scriptures daily as they evaluated the preaching and teaching of the Apostle Paul. They must be willing, by the grace of God and the enablement of the Holy Spirit, to submit to the Lord in all things.

To that end, David James has written an excellent book that will encourage every believer who reads it to grow in discernment at a time when that is greatly lacking among those who profess to be biblical Christians. If anyone thinks this is simply a critique of a popular book that has reached the top of the New York Times best-seller list, he will miss the true value of what James has written. It's a short but very full course on biblical discernment that is a lesson to all of us on how we should evaluate everything we read that claims to teach about the things of God. James underscores Isaiah's admonition regarding discernment: "To the law and the testimony: if they speak not according to [God's] word, it is because there is no light in them" (Isaiah 8:20, KJV).

Not only is this an exceptional volume that covers how we are to implement Jude's exhortation to "earnestly contend for the faith which was once delivered unto the saints" (Jude 3), but James continually demonstrates throughout this book the Apostle Paul's instruction to Timothy of how we are to go about correcting error as servants of the Lord: "And the servant of the Lord must not strive; but be gentle unto all men, apt to teach, patient, In meekness instructing those that oppose themselves; if God peradventure will give them repentance to the acknowledging of the truth; And that they may recover themselves out of the snare of the devil, who are taken captive by him at his will" (2 Timothy 2:24-26).

It is our prayer that you will be greatly edified by what David James has written.

For the Berean Call,

T. A. McMahon
Executive Director

PREFACE

THE HARBINGER is unquestionably a publishing phenomenon of 2012. Perhaps no other book since Hal Lindsey's *The Late Great Planet Earth* has gained so much national attention while challenging its readers with the need to be spiritually prepared for the coming judgment of God. As of this writing, it has been on Amazon.com's top-100 list for more than five months and is rated at number 21 in sales rank of all books of 2012.

As I read the book I was impressed with Cahn's passion for seeing America turn to the Lord, both as a nation and as individuals. Much of the book deals with a number of major events and issues of national and international consequence, including the economy, politics, security, public policy, and the increasing hostility toward God and the Bible. At the same time, the author is careful to emphasize that none of the much-needed change in America can take place apart from spiritual change in individual hearts. On this important matter Cahn gets it exactly right.

Along this line, there have been many reports of those who have dedicated or rededicated their lives and those who have come to faith in the Lord. I am thankful for all who have been moved to consider their relationship with the Lord and to make important spiritual decisions as a result of reading *The Harbinger*. In this regard, Cahn has achieved exactly what he set out to do, and I commend him for that without reservation.

As of this writing, the author and I have not met, but we have corresponded on several occasions. On April 4, 2012, I also had the privilege of engaging in a personal discussion with him by phone that was moderated by Jimmy DeYoung (and is available for listening on ProphecyToday.com). I deeply appreciated Rabbi Cahn's kind and thoughtful interaction, even when discussing certain points of genuine concern. One listener, a long-time pastor and good theologian, commented to me afterward that our discussion was a great example of the way brothers in Christ should handle difficult subjects and areas of disagreement, especially in a public forum. I was very thankful to hear this because that was our desire going into the conversation, and afterward I, too, felt that we had succeeded.

Although I have serious concerns about many things in *The Harbinger*, this critique is not about the author's character, integrity, motives, or sincerity. And even though Jonathan Cahn and I clearly have some well-defined differences on a variety of points, this is not personal in any way.

The purpose of this book is to bring attention to the fact that there is a better way to understand the biblical and historical evidence that Cahn has presented to support his views. My desire is to provide additional information and another perspective so that the reader will be able to more accurately discern the validity of the author's interpretation of the Bible, his views concerning ancient and recent historical events, and his conclusions about the relationship between the two.

How This Book Came to Be Written

On January 6, 2012, I received an email from Jimmy DeYoung (*Prophecy Today*), which contained a link to a segment of the January 3, 2012, *700 Club* program in which Pat Robertson interviewed messianic rabbi Jonathan Cahn about his new book *The Harbinger*, which had been released that day. Based on the interview, Jimmy sensed that there might be cause for concern about the way the author was handling certain Bible passages and connecting biblical prophecy to current events.

I quickly read the book through once so that Jimmy and I could discuss it on his weekly radio program. After reading just the first few pages I began to see why Jimmy was concerned, and the more I read, the more concerned I became. I asked two other trusted men if they would also read the book and give me their impressions (but did not discuss my concerns). After reading *The Harbinger*, their observations and concerns were virtually identical to mine.

Initially I planned to write only a brief four- to six-page review of *The Harbinger*. However, the more I studied and interacted with the book, the longer the review became due to the extent of the problems I was encountering, all of which I have documented extensively.

The Harbinger: Fact or Fiction? is not a book that I set out to write, but it has become clear that it is a book that needed to be written. The importance of responding to *The Harbinger* has been underscored by the fact that after more than five months it continues to ride high on various best-seller lists, including Amazon.com, where it consistently has ranked at or near the top of both the "Christian Fiction" and "Christian Theology" categories. A companion two-hour documentary featuring Jonathan Cahn has also been produced, which has been a top-selling video in its category as well.

The vast majority of reviews across the Internet are overwhelmingly positive. They reflect consistent agreement with Cahn's conclusions, including that it would be impossible for coincidence to explain the number of exact matches between Isaiah 9:10 and events of the last decade in America. Because of these, most also accept the author's interpretation of Isaiah 9:10 as necessarily being correct as well.

Interestingly, a surprising number of conservative evangelical voices have also enthusiastically embraced and promoted *The Harbinger*. I was not expecting to encounter such great differences between other conservative evangelicals and myself, since that very rarely if ever happens. In fact, prior to *The Harbinger* issue, I think we very likely would have all mutually supported one another's views on the vast majority of theological and practical matters.

A troubling development is that Mormon researchers and historians have begun to refer to *The Harbinger* as support for their view that America is in a covenant relationship with God—being the Promised Land and a New Israel. This view, known as Anglo-Israelism, is very much on the fringes if not outside of historical Christianity to the degree that it has been one of the defining characteristics of some cultic groups.

Concerning the significant number of amazingly precise corresponding events proposed by Cahn: If they really *had* occurred in both ancient Israel and in America, it would be rather difficult to dismiss them and provide a reasonable alternative explanation. However, closer examination reveals that in reality the proposed precise matches do not actually exist.

Perhaps the best illustration of what is happening is an optical illusion. Optical illusions cause people to think they are seeing something that doesn't correspond to reality—and such illusions can be very convincing. Straight lines appear to be curved, stationary objects appear to rotate, circles appear to be spirals, objects appear to be larger than they are, and so on.

Optical illusions are created by manipulating the visual context to influence the way things are perceived. With the addition of certain elements, reality can be hidden, obscured, or distorted. The illusion remains convincing until the misleading elements are removed or hidden themselves. Until this is done, it can be difficult to convince people that they are not seeing what they think they are.

I'm not suggesting that Cahn has intentionally mishandled the biblical text or manipulated the evidence in order to deceive or mislead. Although there has been some strong reaction to what little criticism *The Harbinger* and its author have received, this book is not intended to be an attack against another brother in Christ in any way. This is not a personal matter. I have no reason to challenge or question Jonathan Cahn's character, his motives, or his sincerity.

I hope this critique will not be perceived as "majoring on the minors," focusing on insignificant minutiae, and missing the forest for the trees. I fully understand and very much appreciate the overall message of *The Harbinger*, which is that America is on a path of destruction unless there is widespread repentance and a radical turn toward God. The United States may very well already be under God's judgment—and if not, such judgment may not be far away. The situation is serious, and such warnings must be given with passion and clarity.

I do hope that my book will be helpful for a broad spectrum of readers—including those who have enthusiastically supported *The Harbinger*, those who have recognized that there are some significant problems, and those who have not yet decided for sure what they think about the book.

—*David James* (AUGUST, 2012)

THE FIRST ONE TO PLEAD HIS CAUSE SEEMS RIGHT,
UNTIL HIS NEIGHBOR COMES AND EXAMINES HIM.

—Proverbs 18:17

CHAPTER 1

INTRODUCTION

"The bricks have fallen down,
But we will rebuild with hewn stones;
The sycamores are cut down,
But we will replace them with cedars."

—*Isaiah 9:10*

THE HARBINGER, by Jonathan Cahn,[1] focuses on a set of nine small clay discs, identified as seals, which are said to date from the eighth century B.C. and are connected with a prophecy of judgment against Israel in the book of Isaiah (Isaiah 9:10-11). In the story, the original purpose of the seals was to authenticate that Isaiah's message was genuinely from God. Their purpose in the present, however, is to reveal an ancient mystery hidden in the Isaiah passage and to confirm that this revelation also comes from God.

The nine seals are given individually over a period of time to journalist Nouriel Kaplan by a mysterious figure identified only as "The Prophet."[2] Kaplan and The Prophet are the primary characters in the book. Ana Goren, a Manhattan publishing executive to whom Kaplan tells the story of his encounters with The Prophet, also plays a role.

Although Cahn uses a fictional narrative as a framework, the book is based on what he believes are undeniable facts from the biblical text, the corresponding history of eighth century B.C. Israel, and current events of the last decade in America. As Cahn states at the beginning of the book, "What you are about to read is presented in the form of a story, but what is contained within the story is real."[3]

What is real about the story is that the author believes he has discovered nine signs, or omens ("harbingers"), and an ancient mystery in the Isaiah passage that "explains everything from 9/11 to the collapse of the global economy."[4] Furthermore, he believes that these same nine harbingers have appeared once again in America[5] beginning with the 2001 terrorist attacks. Based on Cahn's arguments and massive amount of "evidence," the reader is to conclude that it would be impossible for all of this to have happened by mere coincidence—and therefore the only reasonable explanation is that God must have orchestrated everything.

The overall purpose of *The Harbinger* is to explain that an ancient mystery revealed by these harbingers is a call to America to repent for rejecting God and abandoning the foundations upon which the country was built. The mystery therefore also warns of the imminent danger of God's judgment if this call is ignored.

Make no mistake—calling America back to God is a valid message and one that needs to be proclaimed. America is clearly in trouble in many ways. Cahn rightly points out that "Judgment isn't ultimately about nations—but people. . . . And no one is exempt. Each must stand before Him."[6] He thus challenges his readers to understand that what is even more important than a nation facing *temporal* judgment is that those who do not turn to Christ are facing *eternal* judgment. Jonathan Cahn is to be commended for his passion and commitment to sharing this message with as wide an audience as possible.

However, because of serious flaws throughout the book, its potential dangers may outweigh the benefits. The errors may well overshadow the truth. Many of the views and ideas presented in *The Harbinger* have both significant exegetical and theological problems. The book may leave many of its readers with serious misunderstandings about how to appropriately interpret and apply the Word of God. Another concern is that in trying to support his conclusions Cahn appears to overstate his case, sees prophetic fulfillment where none exists, and presses details to draw parallels between historical events beyond what the facts reasonably support.

The Harbinger not only fails to reveal a mystery in Isaiah 9:10, as it purports to do, but its argument rests on faulty theology, poor methods of interpretation, and inaccurate handling of historical facts. In some cases the book is actually misleading. When studied closely, each of the proposed parallels between the events proves to be very tenuous at best and in most cases nonexistent. The "overwhelming evidence" that so many seem to have uncritically accepted simply evaporates upon closer inspection.

In total, the evidence is like a mirage that is deceptively inviting from a distance but disappears the closer one gets. Therefore, in spite of the much-needed call to repentance, the combination of all the serious problems in the book presents a very real danger to believers and unbelievers alike.

A RUNAWAY SUCCESS

Released on January 3, 2012, *The Harbinger* has already established its place as one of the best-selling books of 2012. According to *CharismaNews*, on January 22 *The Harbinger* debuted at number 10 on the *New York Times* best-seller list in the "print paperback" category and at number 28 in the "combined print hardcover and paperback" category. In just 10 days, it had already been printed four times.

As of June 2, months after its debut on Amazon.com, *The Harbinger* was still ranked at number 1 in the "Christian Fiction" category, at number 1 in "Christian Mystery," and at number 2 in the "Christian Theology" category. *The Harbinger* was also ranked at number 28 for all books, up from number 50 just over a month earlier. On the same date, a total of 438 reader reviews had been entered on Amazon.com—with 349 reviewers giving it a five-star rating and less than 10 percent giving it one star.[7]

The founder of *WorldNetDaily* (now *WND*), Joseph Farah, has produced a two-hour documentary featuring Jonathan Cahn called *The Isaiah 9:10 Judgment*. On April 24, an email alert from *WND* had the following announcement concerning the documentary:

> It was just a few days ago that the epic movie *The Ten Commandments*, starring Charlton Heston as Moses, was ranked as the No. 1 best-selling faith movie at Amazon.
>
> In fact, it [*The Harbinger*] has eclipsed *The Ten Commandments* multiple times since it was released last month to nationwide acclaim. And it's back up as the No. 1 faith video or TV show at Amazon and the No. 5 documentary of any kind.

Nor was this video losing any ground as of June 2. On Amazon.com, the *The Isaiah 9:10 Judgment* DVD set was ranked at number 6 in "Movies & TV/DVD/Documentary" and number 1 in the "Movies & TV/DVD/ Faith & Spirituality" category.

On the day of the book's release, Jonathan Cahn was interviewed by Pat Robertson on *The 700 Club*, who said of the book, "This is one great book. . . . This is the read you need to make. . . . It is a prophetic word."[8] When he appeared on *The Jim Bakker Show*, Bakker said, "I believe with all my heart this is the most important message I have ever brought in my fifty years of broadcasting to a worldwide audience."

In addition to *The 700 Club* and *The Jim Bakker Show*, Cahn has been featured on a number of other programs, including TBN's *Praise the Lord*, Sid Roth's *It's Supernatural,* and Daystar's *Celebration*, giving the book and his ideas exposure to potentially millions of viewers.

Because of the book's astounding success and Cahn's far-reaching influence on so many people already, there is a need for a closer look at *The Harbinger*. One might wonder why such a detailed analysis and critique is necessary for a fictional work. As Jonathan Cahn has noted, however, *The Harbinger* is much more than just fiction. He wrote, "what is contained within the story is real." Therefore, its claims need to be carefully examined.

A Caution Concerning Coincidences

One of the critical premises of *The Harbinger* is that because of the overwhelming number of coinciding events, they cannot be *coincidences*, with the only alternative explanation being that these things *must* have been orchestrated by God. This is probably the single most-repeated argument this author has read on the internet by those commenting on book reviews and articles about the book. Not only is Cahn's explanation viewed as the best plausible one—many, if not most proponents of the book argue that his explanation is the only one that is even possible.

As will be shown in the pages to follow, almost none of the events even coincide, let alone show evidence of being coordinated directly by the hand of God. However, if only for the sake of argument it were accepted that these events do coincide, does that necessarily mean that God's direct intervention is the only possible solution? The following two sets of coincidences demonstrate that Cahn's explanation is not necessarily the only plausible one—because truly amazing coincidences can and do happen.

Lincoln and Kennedy assassinations

This one is an old story, but worth recounting because it is so unusual. It revolves around an unusual number of coincidences that occurred between Presidents Kennedy and Lincoln in regards to their assassination.

For example, both men were elected 100 years apart (Lincoln in 1860, Kennedy in 1960); they were both succeeded by Southerners named Johnson, and the two Johnsons were born 100 years apart (Andrew in 1808, Lyndon in 1908). Both assassins were born 100 years apart (Booth in 1839 and Oswald in 1939) and both died before they could be brought to trial. Lincoln was shot in a theater and his assassin was cornered in a warehouse, while Kennedy was shot from a warehouse and his assassin was captured in a theater. Finally, Lincoln was shot in Ford's theater, while Kennedy was shot while riding in a Ford Lincoln, and to top it all off, Kennedy had a secretary named Lincoln (Evelyn Lincoln) while Lincoln had a secretary named Kennedy.[9]

The Titanic and the Titan

In what has to be considered one of the truly spooky coincidences of all time, in 1898, author Morgan Robertson (1861-1915) wrote a novella entitled *Futility*, or *The Wreck of the Titan,* in which he outlined the voyage of a British luxury liner, HMS *Titan*, that hits an iceberg while crossing the northern Atlantic and sinks with a large loss of life—in part, due to the lack of sufficient lifeboats onboard.

The similarities between the fictional story and the real-life loss of the luxury liner with very nearly the same name 14 years later was extraordinary: both the fictional *Titan* and the real *Titanic* were triple-screw luxury ships about 800 feet long that hit an iceberg in the month of April while traveling at around

25 knots, resulting in the death of some 2,500 souls. Though not identical in every detail (in Robertson's story, the *Titan* capsizes and sinks quickly, while the *Titanic* remained upright and sank slowly over the course of a couple of hours), the similarities are nothing if not amazing.[10]

These are just two of dozens of such stories to be found on many different websites. Does this prove that God didn't orchestrate the events since 9/11 as outlined in *The Harbinger*? No, not at all. But they do represent a cautionary tale that does suggest that believers need to be careful about assigning God's actions to specific events with absolute certainty apart from special revelation from Him.

This is not at all to suggest that believers should not specifically pray for the Lord to intervene in specific circumstances and through specific events. Neither does it mean that His people should not give thanks and praise to Him when he answers those prayers. All should—continually. It is also completely appropriate (because it is biblical) to acknowledge His sovereignty and recognize His providential care in every situation because of His absolute power and immeasurable loving-kindness.

He is not a God who is far away. Rather, He is intimately involved in the affairs of this world.

CHAPTER 2

DEPARTURE FROM A BIBLICAL HERMENEUTIC

A HERMENEUTIC is a set of principles used in interpreting the Bible. At the heart of a biblical hermeneutic is the commitment to understanding a passage in its literary and historical context. It is in this regard that Cahn's thesis first runs into trouble.

LITERAL, GRAMMATICAL, HISTORICAL INTERPRETATION

The literal, grammatical, historical approach to interpreting Scripture is rooted in the idea that the meaning of any given passage resides exclusively in the inspired text itself, which is the very Word of God. The question is not, "What does this mean to me?" Rather it is, "What did this mean to the original author, and what does it mean to God?" It is therefore the interpreter's task to discover that meaning by analyzing the grammar, syntax, and vocabulary of the passage, as well as the overall literary context in which it exists.

The "historical" aspect of a biblical hermeneutic includes the identity of the author and recipients, the time of the writing and of the events, as well as the religious, economic, political, and cultural setting. The historical context does not affect the meaning directly but does provide helpful insights into how it may have been understood by the original readers and how it might be applied today, among other things.

CONTEXTUAL PROBLEMS

The application of a biblical hermeneutic to Isaiah 9:10 reveals nothing that would indicate that either Isaiah or the Lord intended for the prophecy to be understood as having to do with anything other than the Northern Kingdom of Israel in the eighth century B.C. In a moderated discussion on *Prophecy Today* with this author,[1] Cahn affirmed his belief that Isaiah 9:10 was specifically to ancient Israel. He has also stated that the prophecy is not to, for, or about America. This would be consistent with the view of conservative scholars, who generally agree that America is not referenced or in view in any biblical passage. However, the book leaves the reader with the very distinct impression that Isaiah's prophecy and ancient Israel are indeed connected to modern-day America in some way.

One serious departure from using a biblical hermeneutic is the failure to mention the preceding verses in the chapter. These verses form a critical part of the immediate context of Isaiah 9:10 and represent one of the most important messianic kingdom passages in the entire Old Testament. This is a significant omission when dealing with the subject of Israel's judgment because it includes the unconditional promise that even in the face of the coming destruction, Israel's future is still sure. Isaiah 9:1-7 guarantees that the kingdom will still be established and that Messiah will rule from the throne of David forever. It is impossible to understand and apply Isaiah 9:10 correctly unless these verses are brought into the discussion.

Another significant problem is Cahn's view that Isaiah 9:10-11 reflects a *pattern* of God's judgment. In interviews he frequently refers to this pattern as a "template for God's judgment." Based on this theory, he contends that the nine theoretical harbingers coincide precisely with recent historical events, beginning with the terrorist attacks of September 11, 2001.

There is nothing, however, in the immediate context—nor in the context of the entire Bible—that would support this theory. If it is a pattern of God's judgment, then why is it not identified as such, either here or anywhere else in Scripture? If it is a predictable and identifiable pattern, as the author suggests, why is there neither a precedent nor repetition of the pattern in the Bible? Why is this pattern never the subject of any other prophecy? There is simply no biblical warrant for this being identified as a pattern or a template.

A FULLER MEANING?

There is a long-standing debate among biblical scholars as to whether some passages may have a fuller meaning than understood or intended by the human author as his writing was inspired by the Holy Spirit.[2] Even in the case of passages where this might be argued, however, it is only because of later revelation in Scripture that a fuller sense can be suggested at all. Apart from special revelation, there is no biblical basis for interpreting a given passage as having such a fuller sense. To do so is to move into the realm of pure speculation.

Yet as the story develops, one gets the sense that Cahn may believe and is perhaps suggesting that Isaiah 9:10-11 has a fuller, or deeper, meaning—perhaps with some form of dual prophetic fulfillment in view. At the very least he seems to be saying that Isaiah's words are now being reapplied to America, even if that was not originally intended:

> [THE PROPHET] "In the wake of their calamity, the leaders of ancient Israel proclaimed, 'We will rebuild'—the first sign of defiance. *If the mystery holds and has now applied to America, we would expect to hear the same vow*, the same three words, in the wake of 9/11, now proclaimed by American leaders."
>
> [KAPLAN] "And did it happen? Did they say it?"
>
> [THE PROPHET] "Yes. They said it."[3]

* * *

> [GOREN] "How could an ancient mystery possibly have anything to do with September 11?"
>
> [KAPLAN] "*An ancient mystery behind everything from* 9/11 to the economy . . . to the housing boom . . . to the war in Iraq . . . to the collapse of Wall Street. Everything in precise detail."[4]

Throughout the book are many other examples like this in line with *The Harbinger*'s subtitle: *The Ancient Mystery That Holds the Secret of America's Future*. Where is this mystery to be found? According to Cahn, it is in Isaiah 9:10-11. Furthermore, if it was a mystery until it was recently revealed by Jonathan Cahn, then that means it is not obvious from the grammar, syntax, and vocabulary of the passage itself. Again, this suggests that some sort of fuller sense must be in view.

As stated before, any identification of a fuller sense, if it does exist, would require later revelation from God to confirm and justify such an interpretation. Yet there is no such scriptural support for a fuller meaning or a dual fulfillment for the passage in question. Neither in the immediate context nor in any other passage is there any indication that the prophecy could or should be applied to any nation besides Israel—and particularly not to the United States in the twenty-first century.

Therefore, if the meaning of a passage does not come from the text itself or from another passage that explains it, then it must come from outside the Bible. Of course it is not uncommon for people to engage in "eisegesis," or "reading a meaning into a passage." But conservative scholars uniformly reject such methods of interpretation, as undoubtedly would Jonathan Cahn—at least in theory.

This essentially leaves only one other possibility: the author believes that in some way God has revealed this mystery to him or has at least confirmed that his interpretation and conclusions are correct. This will be discussed in a later chapter.

CHAPTER 3

THEN A PROPHECY, NOW A SIGN

AS NOTED in the previous chapter, *The Harbinger* gives the very distinct impression that although the prophecy of Isaiah 9:10 is specifically to Israel, it is not *exclusively* to Israel. Cahn conveys the idea that this verse is also connected to America in some way. Yet as has also been previously noted, Cahn has stated that he is not suggesting this at all. In personal correspondence he has said that those who interpret *The Harbinger* as saying this have misunderstood him.

He has tried to clarify his position (and the apparent discrepancy) by saying that he sees the passage as merely a "sign" to America, not a prophecy. He references the following statement from chapter 6 when he first mentions the issue of the verse being a sign:

> [THE PROPHET] "The prophecy, in its context, concerned ancient Israel. But now, as a sign, it concerns America."[1]

This is not a meaningful distinction and it does not alleviate the problem. Biblical signs are always revelatory and are usually directly connected to the fulfillment of prophecy—and they often prophesy judgment.

SIGNS AND PROPHECIES: THE BIBLICAL CONNECTION

Two well-known examples of the connection between signs and prophecies are found in Isaiah 7 and Matthew 24.

Isaiah 7:14 —

Therefore the Lord Himself will give you a sign: Behold, the virgin shall conceive and bear a Son, and shall call His name Immanuel.

In context, the future virgin birth of a son would be a *sign* to the House of David that the prophecy of God's judgment was being fulfilled. Although Jesus' birth was a miracle, if it had not also fulfilled a *prophecy* of judgment, no one could have known that it was a *sign* of judgment.

Matthew 24:29–30 —

Immediately after the tribulation of those days the sun will be darkened, and the moon will not give its light; the stars will fall from heaven, and the powers of the heavens will be shaken. Then the sign of the Son of Man will appear in heaven, and then all the tribes of the earth will mourn, and they will see the Son of Man coming on the clouds of heaven with power and great glory.

Just as the first coming of Christ was a sign to Israel, His second coming will be a sign to everyone that the prophecies of God's judgment are being *fulfilled*. As immeasurably significant as Christ's return will be, if it would not also fulfill *prophecies* of judgment, no one could know that it was a *sign* of judgment.

This represents an important distinction. In the absence of a prophecy of judgment, Christ's appearing could not be interpreted with any certainty as a *sign* of judgment. This would not be recognized or understood until *after* it became clear that He was executing the judgment. Some might even speculate that His appearance is a sign, but no one could *know* that it is a sign apart from special revelation. Without a preceding prophecy, it could be given any speculative interpretation with no arbiter between differing interpretations until after the fact.

When the Pharisees asked Jesus to give them a sign, they wanted revelatory evidence to prove that He was who He claimed to be. Each time they made such a demand, it was in the context of Jesus speaking about judgment.

Matthew 12:36–38—

> But I say to you that for every idle word men may speak, they will give account of it in the day of judgment. For by your words you will be justified, and by your words you will be condemned. Then some of the scribes and Pharisees answered, saying, "Teacher, we want to see a sign from You."

Another one of the best-known signs in the Bible is part of this same exchange between Jesus and the Pharisees—the "sign of Jonah":

Matthew 12:39–41—

> But He answered and said to them, "An evil and adulterous generation seeks after a sign, and no sign will be given to it except the sign of the prophet Jonah. For as Jonah was three days and three nights in the belly of the great fish, so will the Son of Man be three days and three nights in the heart of the earth. The men of Nineveh will rise up in the judgment with this generation and condemn it, because they repented at the preaching of Jonah; and indeed a greater than Jonah is here."

Obviously the sign of Jonah is associated with Jesus' resurrection, but does it follow the same pattern as discussed above concerning the connection between signs and prophecies? In fact it does.

God had called Jonah to prophesy against Assyria. When Jonah refused the call, he was "buried" in the depths of the sea in the belly of the great fish. Three days later he was "resurrected" to complete his prophetic mission. Therefore, this event functioned as a *sign* that God's judgment had not been abrogated and could only be averted by repentance. So, too, Jesus' resurrection was a sign that the prophecies of God's coming judgment would still be fulfilled in spite of His death.

In each of the above examples, the signs are directly and inseparably connected to the related prophecies. It would seem that Cahn also correctly understands this connection because he handles the harbingers in the same way in his book. This further suggests that he also understands that they can only be signs if they are directly connected with a prophecy.

An Untenable Distinction

In the following exchange, the author attempts to maintain the untenable distinction between Isaiah 9:10 as a prophecy to ancient Israel years ago in contrast to its being a sign to present-day America:

> [KAPLAN] "So what does all this have to do with America?"
>
> [THE PROPHET] "The prophecy, in its context, concerned ancient Israel. But now, as a sign, it concerns America."
>
> [KAPLAN] "How?"
>
> [THE PROPHET] "It's the sign of a nation that once knew God but then fell away, a sign that America is now the nation in danger of judgment . . . and now given warning and the call to return."
>
> [KAPLAN] "So it was originally given to Israel, but now it's given as a sign to America?"
>
> [THE PROPHET] "Yes."[2]

God gave a prophetic word through Isaiah to ancient Israel as a warning of judgment. Cahn believes that God has now revealed that Isaiah's words have become a sign to warn America of impending judgment. However, this distinction is only one of semantics, not of substance.

That the author sees the prophetic force of the harbingers is evident a couple of paragraphs later:

> [KAPLAN] "So if that word should be manifested in America, it becomes a harbinger of America's future?"
>
> [THE PROPHET] "A harbinger," he answered, "and more than one."
>
> [KAPLAN] "The Nine Harbingers."
>
> [THE PROPHET] "Yes. The Nine Harbingers—each one joined to the ancient prophecy, each one joined to this word, and *each one carrying a revelation*. If these harbingers of Israel's judgment

should now reappear, along with this prophetic word, then the nation in which they reappear is in danger."

[KAPLAN] "And you're saying that they have reappeared."

[THE PROPHET] "Yes."[3]

Are the harbingers each "carrying a revelation?" This is precisely what prophecies do. When Israel witnessed an event that was foretold in the prophecy, the event was a sign that prophecy was being fulfilled. This is the way biblical signs always function.

Furthermore, Cahn says that they are appearing in conjunction with exactly the same prophetic word from Isaiah. So in spite of the author's claims to the contrary, there is no difference between the function of Isaiah 9:10 as a prophecy to ancient Israel and the way Cahn is using it in connection with modern-day America. The distinction he is attempting to make between that verse being "a prophecy then" and "a sign now" cannot be maintained.

This is also demonstrably disingenuous and misleading as is evident from his appearance on *The Jim Bakker Show*. He unmistakably reveals his belief that recent events in America were prophesied in Isaiah 9:

It's an over two-and-a-half-thousand-year-old mystery that lies behind everything from 9/11, to the War on Terror, to the economic collapse, to the Great Recession, to the crashes of Wall Street, to what's still happening now that still affects our pocketbooks. And it's something specific—so specific that it actually *ordains the words that American leaders speak out of their mouths.*[4]

CHAPTER 4

A PROPHETIC MESSAGE

EVEN IF RECENT EVENTS in America were to exactly parallel ancient historical events, it is a logical fallacy to conclude that they are necessarily connected. Although a certain set of historical events can be properly attributed to God's judgment if He has revealed this in Scripture, we cannot conclude that similar (or even identical) events must also be attributed to God's judgment—unless He has also revealed this to be the case. For example, even though God judged Egypt through a locust plague, the fact that another region of the world also experiences a swarm of locusts does not necessarily mean that those people are also under God's judgment.

So, does the author believe that the "ancient mystery" and the connection between ancient Israel and America has been recently revealed by God? Given that a prophet is a central character in *The Harbinger*, does Cahn believe that the office of prophet (as held by Isaiah, Jeremiah, Ezekiel, and Daniel, for example) continues to exist today? And if so, does Jonathan Cahn consider himself a prophet?

Jimmy DeYoung posed exactly these questions to him as the moderator of the discussion on April 4, 2012.[1] Cahn never actually gave a clear answer to the question about the contemporary office of prophet. Rather, he simply noted that he tends to be cautious about those who would claim to be prophets or to speak for the Lord.

In answering the second question, as to whether or not the author considers himself a prophet who is speaking for God today, he said:

> I don't claim to be a prophet. I'm just a guy. I'm just me. And no, I don't in any way . . . I'm, you know, very cautious when people speak in those terms. But what I would say is I believe

that the message is a prophetic message in the sense that I believe that in the same way that God can send warning in our lives—and God can send warning to a nation—I believe it is prophetic in that sense.

In an interview on July 3, 2012, Brannon Howse asked Cahn a series of questions because of his concerns about a number of issues in *The Harbinger*. Among these was whether Cahn believes there are still apostles and prophets today. Cahn gave qualified answers about being careful but implied that he would not exclude the possibility. Neither would he comment on whether he thought some in the New Apostolic Reformation who claimed to be apostles and prophets might possibly be false teachers.[2]

Although Cahn says that he does not claim to be a prophet, he does affirm that his message is prophetic. But what else besides "prophet" would be an appropriate title for someone who believes he has discovered the hidden meaning of a biblical mystery that God has given for today and then proclaims this prophetic message as factual? He is doing more than simply *relaying* words given by someone else. He is also doing more than *proclaiming* a hard-hitting message from a passage of Scripture—which could be called prophetic in the general sense that someone is faithfully conveying God's Word. Rather, he is the *originator of a new prophetic message*, revealing things that have never been heard before.

This is even more problematic because Isaiah 9:10 is a prophecy with a meaning that is already clear from the context. By declaring it to contain a hidden mystery, Cahn has given it a private interpretation, which is explicitly unbiblical.

2 Peter 1:19–21—

And so we have the prophetic word confirmed, which you do well to heed as a light that shines in a dark place, until the day dawns and the morning star rises in your hearts; knowing this first, that no prophecy of Scripture is of any private interpretation, for prophecy never came by the will of man, but holy men of God spoke as they were moved by the Holy Spirit.

Peter's words could hardly be more clear. Then on what authority has Cahn given the world this new prophetic message based on Isaiah's already-clear prophecy?

In an interview with Molly Noble Bull of *Commandment Keepers* on May 13, 2012, he affirmed what he believes is the supernatural origin of *The Harbinger* as well as how the publishing of the book was itself prophetic fulfillment.

> [MOLLY] Many of our readers are published authors or trying hard to get published for the first time. Yet you said in your interviews that you never intended to become a writer—that the Lord told you to write *The Harbinger*. Later, you prayed and still more amazing things took place with regard to the sale of the book. Please tell us all about those amazing events.
>
> [JONATHAN] *The Harbinger* just flowed out and was finished in a few months time. The week I finished it, I was scheduled to speak at Promise Keepers in Dallas. My flight took me to Charlotte, North Carolina. There I prayed, "Lord, *The Harbinger* is your message. I don't want it to go forth by the ways of man. It's yours. You get out the word Your way."
>
> I opened my eyes. There was a man sitting next to me. He begins to speak to me. Then he begins to prophesy over me.
>
> He tells me I will publish a book, and more than one—that God is about to do something big, and it will change my life. It turns out that before we met, the man was just brought together with the president of Charisma Media, Steve Strang. He sends word to him.
>
> A little while later, I received contact from Steve Strang, telling me he heard what happened at the airport. He heard about *The Harbinger*, and he's interested.
>
> That's how *The Harbinger* became published—not by the plans or hand of men, but totally supernaturally. In fact, that whole scene at the airport was as a recreation of a scene in the book where a man meets "a prophet."[3]

PROMOTIONS AND ADVERTISEMENTS

That Cahn is being presented as a modern-day prophet seems readily apparent. For example, in a brief biography about the author, the back cover of *The Harbinger* states:

> His teachings are seen on television and radio throughout the nation and are known for their prophetic significance and their revealing of deep mysteries of God's Word.

In September 2011, the program *It's Supernatural* aired shows that were produced around interviews with Jonathan Cahn. The following are excerpts from an advertisement for a DVD set featuring those shows:

> Rabbi Jonathan Cahn's new book gives a *fresh prophetic Jewish* perspective and insight that clearly shows the future of America. . . .
> And is it possible that God is now sending a *prophetic word to America,* a word of warning that the nation lies in danger and unless it returns to Him is heading for impending judgment?[4]

The same promotional ad says the following of the author:

> Jonathan Cahn is a Jewish believer in Messiah and leader in the Messianic movement. His teachings and messages are *known for their profound and prophetic nature* and for revealing the deep mysteries of biblical truth.

The following is from another website that exclusively promotes *The Harbinger* and an accompanying DVD set:

> Listen as Jonathan Cahn shares *the revelations*, the details, and the significance that lie behind and within the mysteries and *prophetic message* of *The Harbinger*.[5]

In a promotional video for the DVD set, Cahn affirms the prophetic nature of his message (and not simply in the generic sense of being a "forthtelling" of God's Word from Scripture):

> [JONATHAN CAHN] Could there exist an ancient mystery that holds the secret of America's future? And could this mystery touch everything, explain everything from 9/11, to the global war on terror, to Wall Street, to your bank account, to your future, to your well-being? The answer is yes.

> [VOICE-OVER] Call now and receive Rabbi Jonathan Cahn's

two-part *prophetic audio CD revelation* . . .[6]

On Amazon.com, the book description includes the following:

> Hidden in an ancient biblical prophecy from Isaiah, the myster-
> ies revealed in *The Harbinger* are so precise that *they foretold*
> recent American events down to the exact days. The *revela-
> tions are so specific* that even the most hardened skeptics will
> find it hard to dismiss or put down. It sounds like the plot of a
> Hollywood thriller with one exception . . . IT'S REAL.[7]

What Others Are Saying

Sid Roth concludes the first segment of his interview series on *It's
Supernatural* by saying, "This may be—no, this is *the most important
prophetic show you will ever see.*"[8] Later, Roth tells Cahn:

> David Wilkerson was a prophet. You are a prophet that's going
> on really deep revelation of what David Wilkerson saw [*sic*].
> What do you think is going to happen to America?[9]

If ever Cahn were going to deny that he is a prophet, that would have
been the time to do so. Yet not only did he fail to correct Roth, but he also
went on to answer Roth's question, giving his view as to what he sees is
yet ahead for the United States, as if he had accepted what Roth had just
said about him.

Across the Internet, *The Harbinger* is described as conveying a prophetic message. Some specifically identify Cahn as a prophet and as
someone to whom God has given this message:

> I just want to show you a video . . . of Rabbi Jonathan Cahn.
> And he's a Jewish Rabbi. *He's also a prophet.*[10]

* * *

The Pastor wrote this article out of deep conviction by the Holy
Spirit and based on *a prophetic Word from the Lord* given to
Jonathon [*sic*] Cahn in 2005.[11]

* * *

You might call Jonathan Cahn a harbinger—*one who foreshadows what is to come*. The Messianic rabbi's prophetic message is not only winning the attention of the body of Christ, it's beginning to demand . . .[12]

I recently had the opportunity to discuss *The Harbinger* with Cahn. He believes *the Holy Spirit showed him* that events such as 9/11, the collapse of Wall Street, and the Great Recession are the result of God lifting His hedge of protection around America.[13]

Several things seem to emerge fairly clearly:

1. *The Harbinger* is being promoted as a prophetic message, and Jonathan Cahn is being promoted as a prophet.

2. Many readers have been persuaded that the prophecy of Isaiah 9:10 contains a hidden message specifically to the United States.

3. Many have been persuaded that Jonathan Cahn is functioning as a prophet for today and being used by God to reveal this ancient mystery.

4. Cahn himself seems to believe that God has chosen him to reveal the hidden prophetic message of Isaiah to America (because this idea cannot be understood on the basis of the text alone).

CHAPTER 5

THE DAVID WILKERSON CONNECTION

DAVID WILKERSON[1] was well known for his many prophecies of God's coming judgment against America, going back at least to his book *The Vision*, which was published in 1973.[2] He has been widely criticized for many of these prophecies, such as the following one from 1992:

> Thirty days of chastisement will fall on New York City such as the world has never seen. God is going to let down the walls. There will be unimaginable violence and looting. The violence will be so ferocious, it will shock the whole world. Our streets will be lined not just with the National Guard but with militia.
> . . .
> Times Square will be ablaze, and the flames will ascend into heaven and be seen for miles. Fire trucks will not be able to handle it all. . . .
> You may ask, when will all this happen? All I can say is, I believe I will be here when it happens.[3]

Wilkerson died in 2011, and it has been almost 20 years since the prophecy was first given.

Another well-known failed prophecy from 1994 concerned the collapse of Christian broadcasting:

> Right now I sense in my spirit that in less than five years, there will be no more so-called gospel television networks. They will all fall into bankruptcy and absolute ruin. . . .

The only thing left will be some local television programs with true men of God preaching the gospel. And all the phony smiles, the ungodly fund-rasing circuses, the pop theology, the preaching of prosperity are going to come down.[4]

More than ten years have passed since the collapse was to have occurred. Yet these networks continue to thrive and control most of the Christian broadcasting infrastructure.

WILKERSON, CAHN, AND 9/11

As noted in the previous chapter, in the *It's Supernatural* interview, Sid Roth identified Jonathan Cahn as a prophet, comparing him to David Wilkerson. Roth had actually made the connection with Wilkerson early in the interview:

> [ROTH] Jonathan, I was so amazed when I found out that David Wilkerson was saying the same words you were saying, but you have brought clarity to it that anyone could understand.

> [CAHN] Yeah, the, the amazing thing is that he said it the week after 9/11—and it wasn't because he was . . . he was seeing these things; it just came to him from the Lord and he said, "This is the word."[5]

As can be seen, Cahn elaborates on Roth's comments, affirming that David Wilkerson had received a prophetic word from God concerning 9/11—and that Wilkerson genuinely was a prophet. And in the context of these exchanges, Cahn also accepts the connection that Roth makes between Wilkerson and himself as prophets to whom God has shown the same things concerning Isaiah 9:10.

Cahn himself brought up the issue of the identical understanding of Isaiah 9:10 and 9/11 that he and David Wilkerson shared in *The 700 Club* interview with Pat Robertson:

> When 9/11 happens—our ministry is nearby. When it happened, I was drawn to Isaiah 9 and 10. I was praying on that particular point in Israel's history that was linking up to this.

> At the same time—I found out later that David Wilkerson was led that there was *a word for America at the same time, and it was the exact same word, the exact same verse.*[6]

David Wilkerson denied that he was a prophet just as Jonathan Cahn has. Yet he apparently believed that God was speaking through him. As noted earlier, in the September 7, 1992, prophecy concerning God's impending judgment against America, he said, "God is going to let down the wall." However, in a note appended to this message on the referenced website, Wilkerson said that in the wake of the 2001 attacks:

> Calls and messages have flooded our ministry offices, asking, "Was the terrorist attack on September 11 the calamity you were prophesying back in 1992?" No, not at all. What I saw coming will be much more severe.[7]

While Cahn believes that God removed the "hedge of protection" and that there was a "breach in the wall" on 9/11, Wilkerson stated that the terrorist attacks were not the fulfillment of the prophecies concerning the coming breach.

Who is right? Through whom has God spoken? Wilkerson or Cahn? Neither? It can't be both, so at least one of them is wrong. Who decides? Has the Apostle Peter (2 Peter 1:19-21) already provided the answer, since both Wilkerson and Cahn gave private interpretations of Isaiah 9:10?

"No Perfect Prophets"

Such contradictions are not uncommon among contemporary "prophets." Unfortunately in much of the church today the idea of prophets getting it wrong is acceptable. The following perspective is not unusual.

> There are no perfect prophets. There are very few perfect prophecies. I would expect that even experienced prophets get it wrong sometimes. I suspect that most prophets would be very happy, *if they got it right 90 percent of the time.* An even larger percentage of prophecies from God will be slightly contaminated by something the prophet has added from his own heart. This is normal even for experienced prophets, because all prophets are human.[8]

However, the fact that false prophecy carried with it the death penalty reveals that the Lord has a very different view of the matter:

Deuteronomy 18:20–22—

> But the prophet who presumes to speak a word in My name, which I have not commanded him to speak, or who speaks in the name of other gods, that prophet shall die. And if you say in your heart, "How shall we know the word which the LORD has not spoken?"— when a prophet speaks in the name of the LORD, if the thing does not happen or come to pass, that is the thing which the LORD has not spoken; the prophet has spoken it presumptuously; you shall not be afraid of him.

By God's grace, such penalties are no longer in force for anyone today. However, the New Testament equates false teachers with the false prophets of old, giving stern warnings concerning their presence and influence in the church.

2 Peter 2:1–2—

> But there were also false prophets among the people, even as there will be false teachers among you, who will secretly bring in destructive heresies, even denying the Lord who bought them, and bring on themselves swift destruction. And many will follow their destructive ways, because of whom the way of truth will be blasphemed.

John warned of those who would ultimately separate themselves from the fellowship of believers who continue in the teachings of the apostles:

1 John 2:18–19—

> Little children, it is the last hour; and as you have heard that the Antichrist is coming, even now many antichrists have come, by which we know that it is the last hour. They went out from us, but they were not of us; for if they had been of us, they would have continued with us; but they went out that they might be made manifest, that none of them were of us.

That false teachers are to be identified, sent away, and avoided will be discussed in the final section of this chapter.

ZEPHANIAH'S PROPHECY—TO THE CHURCH?

David Wilkerson also believed that at least some prophecies against ancient Israel have a second referent, or fuller meaning, as well—Zephaniah 3:18, for example. According to Wilkerson, Zephaniah's prophecy is also to "spiritual Zion" (in other words, "spiritual Israel," i.e., the Church of Jesus Christ). In his sermon *The Reproach of the Solemn Assembly,* Wilkerson says of Zephaniah 3:18:

> *This is a dual prophecy* by Zephaniah. It has to do with the children of Israel . . . and also with spiritual Zion (which is the church of Jesus Christ of the last day). First of all, he was speaking to Jews—that God was going to gather together the dispersed. . . .
>
> *This prophecy is also to the Church of Jesus Christ* in the Last Day. In the Old Testament, the children of Israel were called to their festivals for seven days. On the eighth day—it was called a Solemn Assembly. . . .
>
> This is the Church of Jesus Christ in the Last Day. According to Zephaniah, the House of God in the Last Days is going to be under reproach . . .[9]

Cahn noted in interviews that Wilkerson saw the same things that he does in Isaiah 9:10 as supporting evidence for the validity of his own conclusions. He remained silent when Sid Roth identified him with David Wilkerson and as a prophet. He did not deny the continuity between his own teachings and Wilkerson's when it was suggested by others but instead elaborated on it. Taken together, David Wilkerson's influence, at least on Cahn's present views, is very evident—and it is problematic.

ACCEPTING THE "PROPHETS" REJECTED BY WILKERSON

Significantly more troubling than Cahn's identification with Wilkerson, however, are his public appearances (largely on television) with a number of people who have demonstrated that they are not simply "less-than-perfect" prophets. Some of these promoters of *The Harbinger* are among the best-known false prophets of this generation. This fact is understood by almost everyone who does not share their heretical views. Even David Wilkerson had consistently spoken out against these false teachers, some of whom represent the most extreme Charismatic excesses. Among these are Sid Roth, Jim Bakker, Pat Robertson, and Perry Stone (on TBN)— false prophets and false teachers whom Cahn has not avoided.

Some might argue that this is a decision only about philosophy of ministry, leaving room for disagreement as a practical matter. However, the following passages should sound the alarm for anyone who might be tempted to dismiss these associations as simply pragmatic ministry decisions that say nothing about Cahn's overall views and the theology underlying *The Harbinger*:

2 John 9—

> Whoever transgresses and does not abide in the doctrine of Christ does not have God. He who abides in the doctrine of Christ has both the Father and the Son. If anyone comes to you and does not bring this doctrine, do not receive him into your house nor greet him . . .

Romans 16:17–18—

> Now I urge you, brethren, note those who cause divisions and offenses, contrary to the doctrine which you learned, and avoid them. For those who are such do not serve our Lord Jesus Christ, but their own belly, and by smooth words and flattering speech deceive the hearts of the simple.

1 Timothy 6:20–21—

> O Timothy! Guard what was committed to your trust, avoiding the profane and idle babblings and contradictions of what is falsely called knowledge—by professing it some have strayed concerning the faith. Grace be with you.

Cahn's problematic ministry decisions since the release of *The*

Harbinger have not been limited to just these interviews and promotions. In April, Cahn was one of the keynote speakers at Chuck Pierce's Celebrate Passover conference. This meant sharing the platform and pulpit with men and women who are leaders in the New Apostolic Reformation (NAR) movement. The NAR is dedicated to promoting doctrines worldwide that are also thoroughly unbiblical and dangerous. That Cahn would minister alongside these "apostles and prophets" does suggest that this is not a significant problem for him. The brief biographies of just a few of the other conference speakers needs no comment.[10]

> Chuck Pierce . . . also serves as President of Global Spheres, Inc., an apostolic ministry for apostolic, prophetic and intercessory leaders. He is known for his accurate prophetic gifting, which helps direct nations, cities, churches and individuals in understanding the times and seasons we live in.

> C. Peter Wagner is the Ambassadorial Apostle of Global Spheres, Inc. (GSI), led by Chuck Pierce. GSI is an apostolic network providing activation and alignment for Kingdom-minded leaders of the Body of Christ. He travels extensively throughout the United States and other nations helping to equip Believers to minister in the areas of apostolic ministries, wealth, dominion, and reformation of society.

> Barbara J. Yoder is the founding apostle and senior pastor of Shekinah Christian Church, a racially and culturally diverse church in Ann Arbor, Michigan. Pastor Barbara is known for her cutting-edge prophetic ministry and apostolic breakthrough anointing.

> Kyle Searcy is a recognized and highly respected, apostle, prayer warrior, teacher, and author. Apostle Kyle . . . serves as Apostle and co-founder . . . Fresh Anointing House of Worship, located in historic Montgomery, Alabama.

Cahn believes that any concern someone might have with associations like this is nothing more than an illegitimate "guilt-by-association" charge. This might be true if there were just an isolated incident here and there, but that is not the case. Most of the highest-profile promotion of *The Harbinger* has come from Cahn's intimate association with these organizations. This is further confirmed by the fact that his publisher is Charisma House. In an open public letter to T. A. McMahon, Cahn not only dismissed this concern but rather ridiculed it and went so far as to suggest that just expressing such concern is a "sin":

> But in the article you do raise one "big red flag" and a "discernment alert" concerning . . . of all things, the book's publisher. You've devoted an entire section to establishing this connection as if it somehow meant something. Here is the logic: Charisma puts out some books that you consider to be erroneous or false. *The Harbinger* is put out by Charisma. Therefore it must be suggested that *The Harbinger* might on these grounds be erroneous or false. . . . It exemplifies one of the key errors such ministries often fall into, namely assigning "guilt by association." In other words, "Since the publisher puts out books we disagree with, this, in itself, gives us the go ahead to publicly raising doubt and suspicions concerning this book.". . . The same "guilt by association" charge is often leveled against other ministers. . . . By such indiscriminate sword-wielding, many good ministers and ministries of God and their reputations can and have been attacked and wounded and major damage inflicted within the kingdom. . . . I believe this is a major sin before God concerning His kingdom before Whom we must stand accountable.[11]

Yes, there is accountability for all. This means that there is also accountability for being in a contractual business relationship with a company that has been built almost exclusively upon publishing, distributing, and actively promoting some of the most extreme of the extreme false teachers in the world. Charisma House has published and *Charisma* magazine has regularly featured such people as Benny Hinn, John Arnott, Mike Bickle, T. D. Jakes, Perry Stone, Reinhard Bonnke, Joyce Meyer, Jim Bakker, Fred Price, Rodney Howard-Browne, Oral Roberts, Joseph Prince, and countless others.

In his open letter to T. A. McMahon, Cahn tells the the story of how Steve Strang, founder of *Charisma* magazine, personally contacted him because Strang had heard of a prophecy given over him in the Charlotte airport (also noted in the previous chapter).[12] Cahn and Strang appeared together on *The Jim Bakker Show* on April 30, 2012, to discuss Cahn's book. It is simply impossible for the author of *The Harbinger* to distance himself from the publisher of his book.[13] Rather than avoiding one of the most influential promoters of false prophets and teachers, Cahn has drawn close to him.

Furthermore, it must be noted as a confirmation that these relationships are not just incidental and inconsequential. In this April 30 appearance, Cahn noted that *The Harbinger* had been launched on *The Jim Bakker Show,* and as a returning guest he said that the show felt like "home" to him.[14] He went on to say that the launching of the book took place on the show on January 2, 2012.

These all point to the fact that Jonathan Cahn has personal and close ministry relationships with these false teachers who are promoting his book. Why he would try to distance himself from these men when speaking and writing to those concerned about the book is puzzling and actually seems rather disingenuous.

CHAPTER 6

FACT OR FICTION?

JONATHAN CAHN has said that he originally intended to write a nonfiction book that would document the things he has discovered about Isaiah 9:10 and ancient Israel as they apply to modern-day America.[1] He was encouraged by others, however, that a novel would make his message more accessible and more widely read. The book's success attests to the value of that advice.

As previously noted, even though categorized as "fiction," the story is prefaced by this statement: "What you are about to read is presented in the form of a story, but what is contained within the story is real."[2] In other words, the book conveys what Cahn considers to be biblically accurate and historically factual, utilizing fiction only as a framework for presenting his message. Because of this approach, it is in some ways similar to a historical novel or a Tom Clancy book. While it is fiction on one level, on another level it is not.

Although it isn't a significant problem in historical novels when the lines between fact and fiction are blurred, such is not the case with *The Harbinger*. With most historical novels, the fictional story is the most important part, with the historical situation and the events providing a framework for telling that story. No one would attempt to use a historical novel as a history book. No one would assume that they were discovering the detailed inner workings of the CIA from a Tom Clancy novel. In the case of *The Harbinger*, the fact-or-fiction question is not at all clear. This is a serious matter.

An example of the lack of a clear "real or imaginary" distinction is the case of the nine harbingers. The story centers around a set of small clay discs that are said to date from the eighth century B.C. and are associated with Isaiah's prophecy. The purpose of the nine seals is to reveal and explain the nine harbingers and the ancient mystery they hold. They are also to authenticate that the message comes from God.

> [THE PROPHET] "Seals like this one were used to mark important documents—edicts, decrees, communications by kings, rulers, princes, priests, and scribes—in ancient times. The seal was the sign of authenticity. It would let you know that the message was real, from someone important, and to be taken seriously."[3]

Do these seals really exist as an archaeological find, or are they simply part of the fictional storyline? The answer is not clear in the book, and many readers may well wonder if the seals are real and actually exist—although they do not.

Why is this important? Because of Cahn's claim that what is in the book is real. It's a legitimate question to ask if these seals are genuine historical artifacts traceable to a prophet of God almost 3,000 years ago. The average person in the U.S. is often not aware of recent archaeological discoveries in the Middle East. If the seals were real, that could be significant concerning the credibility of the entire book. Since the book already has fairly extensive footnotes, it would certainly have been appropriate and helpful to note in that manner that the seals are only a literary device.

As it is, rather than adding an element of authenticity to the story, the nine harbinger seals only serve to confuse matters. The obvious question is, Even though a literary device, does his use of the seals suggest that Cahn believes his views are authentically from God and that He has confirmed this in some other way that is simply *symbolized* by the seals? In the essence of what they represent, are they fact or fiction?

Another such question concerns The Prophet and Nouriel Kaplan. Are they purely fictional characters, or are they based on real people to some degree? The most obvious question is, Did any of *The Harbinger* come from someone who is regarded as a prophet? There is nothing obvious in the story that would help the reader to know whether or not this is part of the story that is "real." The perception that such a person might really exist is reinforced by the significant number of close similarities between Kaplan and the author, as outlined in a later chapter of this book. Although these similarities may be unintentional, they undeniably exist in the story. So, how much of this part of the story is fact, and how much is fiction?

In the second half of the book, Kaplan has a dream about the dedication of the temple in Jerusalem that includes the biblical King Solomon. In the dream, when Solomon turns around, he is unexpectedly transformed into George Washington there on the Temple Mount. The following are excerpts from the encounter with The Prophet after the dream, when Kaplan is searching for answers concerning what he saw.

[KAPLAN] "What happened on April 30?"

[THE PROPHET] "It was the day that the nation's government was completed as set forth in the Constitution, the day America's first president was inaugurated."

[KAPLAN] "George Washington!"

[THE PROPHET] "Yes."

[KAPLAN] "He was part of it too," I said. "He was there in the dream . . . at the dedication of the Temple. First it was King Solomon, and then it was Washington."

* * *

[THE PROPHET] "What was he doing in your dream?"

[KAPLAN] "Leading the people in prayer, like Solomon. And then he stretched out his hand as if reaching for something."

* * *

[THE PROPHET] "He was placing his hand on a Bible," said The Prophet, "to swear. He was taking the oath of the presidency. It was the inauguration, April 30, 1789, the beginning of America as a constituted nation—the foundation, 212 years before 9/11."

[KAPLAN] "The inauguration of George Washington on the Temple Mount?"

[THE PROPHET] "In your dream the two events were joined together—Israel's dedication and America's inauguration, the one superimposed on the other."

[KAPLAN] "Why?"

[THE PROPHET] "It was your dream . . . you tell me."

[KAPLAN] "Because somehow the two days are connected?"

Because of the blending of fact and fiction, it's impossible to know from the storyline whether this dream is just a literary device or if it is based on a dream the author actually had. Although Cahn has stated that he did not have such a dream, the fact that it is a literary device does not mitigate the problems introduced by the concepts it conveys. The Prophet accepts the dream as providing a meaningful interpretation of events in America over the past decade. So to what degree does Cahn actually see a connection between King Solomon and President Washington—or is even the connection itself just a literary device? Based on the story alone, the reader would most naturally conclude that in the author's mind the connection itself is real. Once again, the crucial question for the average reader is: Is this fact or fiction?

Another major issue is the interpretation of events in America since 9/11. Can the author's interpretation of the events rightly be considered facts, as he apparently does? For example, Cahn believes that God removed His "hedge of protection" from the United States, which allowed the successful attacks on the World Trade Center. He also believes that these attacks marked the beginning of God's judgment on the nation.

To claim to know these things with the absolute certainty affirmed by the author is to claim insight into the very mind of God, including His specific purposes and plans for America in this generation. Although one might speculate and form opinions, these things cannot be known for sure unless God personally reveals them. So does Cahn believe that he has received this necessary revelation? And if so, is he right? Is God using him as a prophet? Has God given him special insight into an ancient mystery?

Has God truly shown him that his confidence in the veracity of his interpretation and conclusions is justified? Or does his message amount to nothing more than speculation? Is it fact, or is it fiction?

In the interview on July 3 with Brannon Howse, Cahn noted that *The Harbinger* was 90 percent factual.[5] But the matter of which 10 percent is fiction is critically important. This doesn't necessarily mean that fiction should not be used when dealing with this subject matter, but it does highlight the potential danger of mixing fact and fiction—particularly if the author must explain which is which after the fact.

CHAPTER 7

THE MYSTERY OF ISAIAH 9:10

A Direct Link?

CAHN DENIES arguing for a direct connection between Israel and America and maintains that the passage only demonstrates a *pattern* of God's judgment. He likewise concludes that recent events in America, beginning with 9/11, are only *parallels* to that specific pattern. Yet in multiple places Cahn gives the very clear impression that these are more than simply parallels and that a direct connection does exist. Based on what the author clearly states, it's difficult to conclude that this is not precisely what he intended to convey at the time. The following are a few of the numerous examples:

> [GOREN] "How could an ancient mystery have anything to do with September 11?"

> [KAPLAN] "An *ancient mystery behind everything* from 9/11 to the economy . . . to the housing boom . . . to the war in Iraq . . . to the collapse of Wall Street. *Everything in precise detail.*"[1]

> * * *

> [KAPLAN] "But what does America have to do with ancient Israel?"

[THE PROPHET] "Israel was unique among the nations in that it was conceived and dedicated at its foundation for the purposes of God."

[KAPLAN] "OK..."

[THE PROPHET] "But there was one other—a civilization also conceived and dedicated to the will of God from its conception . . . America. In fact, those who laid its foundations . . ."

[KAPLAN] "The Founding Fathers."

[THE PROPHET] "No, long before the Founding Fathers. Those who laid America's foundations saw it as *the new Israel, an Israel of the New World. And as it was with ancient Israel, they saw it as in covenant with God.*"[2]

* * *

[THE PROPHET] "The Assyrians are the fathers of terrorism, and those who mercilessly plotted out the calamity on 9/11 were their spiritual children, *another link in the mystery joining America to ancient Israel.*"[3]

* * *

[KAPLAN] "So if the ancient mystery is *joined to America*, then somehow 9/11 has to be linked to the words 'We will rebuild.'"[4]

* * *

[THE PROPHET] "Well done, Nouriel. So what would we expect to find in Washington DC?"

[KAPLAN] "Some link between this city and the ancient vow," I said. "*Somehow Isaiah 9:10 has to be connected to Washington DC.*"[5]

* * *

[THE PROPHET] "And all referring to America's campaign to defy the calamity of 9/11, as he *links it all to the judgment of ancient Israel.*[6]

* * *

[THE PROPHET] "Solomon was the king of Israel. Washington was the first president of the United States. There was something in *the linking of ancient Israel and America,* as with all the other mysteries."[7]

Linked. Joined. Connected. Behind everything. Cahn's belief in a direct *prophetic* connection between Isaiah 9:10, Israel, and the United States could not be more clear. As such, the author's theory about this direct connection unambiguously forms the "factual" basis for the entire story.

A DRIVING FORCE?

Not only does Cahn seem to believe there is a connection, but he presents the "hidden mystery" in Isaiah 9:10 as if Isaiah's words became a driving force in events in America over the last decade. Cahn's thinking can be seen when The Prophet directly links Isaiah 9:10 to America's economy through what he will call the *Isaiah 9:10 Effect* (discussed later in this book):

[THE PROPHET] "And since the economic boom was linked to Isaiah 9:10 . . . the Isaiah 9:10 Effect . . . *it ultimately had to collapse.*"[8]

"It ultimately had to collapse" because of the cause/effect relationship that Cahn sees between the words of Isaiah 9:10 and recent events in America. Once the prophecy was triggered by the words spoken by America's leaders, an inevitable cascade of events followed. He clearly reveals that this is his view earlier in the same chapter when he discusses the words of Isaiah 9:10 in terms of it being a vow:

[KAPLAN] "And it all began with the vow."

[THE PROPHET] "It was the vow that set it all in motion . . ."

Cahn explained this cause/effect relationship in *The 700 Club* interview on January 3, 2012:

> [The mystery] even has *determined the actions and the actual words* of American leaders. A mystery that goes back two-and-a-half thousand years and is a warning of judgment and a call of God—a prophetic call of God . . .[9]

Arguing for a cause/effect relationship between the words of Isaiah 9:10 and events in America while denying that it is a prophecy about America comes perilously close to being a mystical view and application of the passage. It almost sounds as if he is suggesting that the power of the prophecy is bound up in the formulaic use of the words themselves.

Although such a use of words is characteristic in certain mystical practices, this is not the way biblical prophecy works. The power of biblical prophecy is not in the words that are spoken but in the Lord who is the source of the prophecy. Cahn undoubtedly understands this, and it seems unlikely that he intended to give the impression that he has given about Isaiah's prophecy. But he would not be the first to unintentionally confuse *biblical* approaches to understanding and applying the Word of God with *mystical* ones.

CHAPTER 8

AMERICA: A NEW ISRAEL?

The Abrahamic Covenant

IN GENESIS 12, Moses records that God personally called one man, Abraham (his name was Abram at the time), to leave his home in the region that is modern-day Iraq and go to the region of modern-day Israel. Through him God would bring forth an entirely new nation and a new people—His chosen people. This new nation would be established on the foundation of a unique covenant with Abraham and his descendants through his son Isaac and his grandson Jacob. Within two more generations, this new nation would be known as "Israel" (as a result of God changing Jacob's name).

Abraham entered into this covenant by faith, forever establishing Israel as a unique nation in a unique relationship with God that would be enjoyed by no other nation. The Abrahamic Covenant is eternal, uncon-ditional, and *unilateral*—meaning that its fulfillment ultimately depends only upon the faithfulness of God.

An American Covenant?

In the moderated discussion of April 4 on *Prophecy Today*, as well as in email correspondence, Jonathan Cahn stated that he does not believe that America is "*The* New Israel" or "*A* New Israel," or that America has replaced Israel in God's program in any way. However, there are a number of exchanges between The Prophet and Nouriel Kaplan that could easily leave *The Harbinger*'s readers with a far different impression—that perhaps there is some sort of "American Covenant" similar to or even related to the Abrahamic Covenant in some way.

This is not simply an incidental issue that can be overlooked as inconsequential. As presented, the argument of the entire book seems to rely on the idea that America's founders had indeed established the new nation to be in a *covenant relationship with God* similar to that of ancient Israel. If it were not for the belief that such a covenant relationship with God does exist in at least some way and that America has failed to remain faithful to that covenant, there would be no basis for the book or for any of Cahn's major ideas.

THE VIEWS OF THE FOUNDERS

Even though the author denies a belief that America is the new Israel or a nation in covenant with God, the founders of America, whom he invokes early on in the book, *did* believe this. As quoted previously, The Prophet builds the case for the connection between the prophecy against Israel in Isaiah 9:10 and events of the last decade in America by referencing the thinking and intentions of America's founders (as noted a few pages earlier):

> [THE PROPHET] "But there was one other—a civilization also conceived and dedicated to the will of God from its conception . . . America. In fact, those who laid its foundations . . ."
>
> [KAPLAN] "The Founding Fathers."
>
> [THE PROPHET] "No, long before the Founding Fathers. Those who laid America's foundations saw it as *the new Israel, an Israel of the New World*. And as it was with ancient Israel, they saw it as in covenant with God."[1]

This exchange makes it clear that even beyond the Founding Fathers, Cahn has the earliest founders in view—that is, the Puritans and Pilgrims.

Nor is this an inconsequential detail because the Puritans were intent upon establishing God's kingdom on earth under the banner of "one nation under God."[2]

Although some have suggested that societal and political concerns were secondary for the Pilgrims,[3] their ultimate goal and perspective does not seem to be significantly different:

> In 1620, long before the United States won its independence from England, the Pilgrims came to America's shores with this mission statement,
>
> "[W]e all came to these parts of America, with one and the same end and aim, namely, to advance the Kingdom of our Lord Jesus Christ." —*New England Confederation of 1643*[4]

In keeping with this, they believed that the prophecies given to ancient Israel could be applied to the new nation that was forming, as well. In other words, ancient Israel and America were connected. A potential reason for this can be seen in the following quote from an article on Endtimepilgrim.org, which refers to the "ten lost tribes of Israel" (the "lost tribes" will be discussed in the next section):

> So our Christian and Puritan dreams for "one nation under God" are probably quite ancient. There may even be some connection between European Christendom and the lost ten tribes of Israel. Hebrew/Australian scholar Yair Davidy, who now resides in Jerusalem, has carefully researched and written extensively on this subject.[5]

This is not the same as classic replacement theology, which says that the church has replaced Israel in God's program. It is clear, however, that the founders saw America as the new central nation in God's kingdom, established through a covenant like that of Abraham, and built on the Law of Moses. And they were doing this as the church. This must be viewed either as a distinct form of replacement theology or perhaps a form of covenant theology (which teaches that there is only one people of God).

As a Messianic Jew who identifies himself as a rabbi of the tribe of Levi and of the house of Aaron,[6] one would think that Cahn would see the problem this presents. And in fact, he has strongly denied that he holds to any type of replacement theology. In spite of this, he actually furthers the perception of embracing this view by presenting America as a "called nation" that is also in covenant with God, as *prophesied* by her founders:

> [THE PROPHET] "Those who laid America's foundations saw it as a new Israel, an Israel of the New World. And as with ancient Israel, *they saw it as in covenant with God.*"
>
> [KAPLAN] "Meaning?"
>
> [THE PROPHET] "Meaning its rise or fall would be dependent on its relationship with God. If it followed His ways, America would become the most blessed, prosperous, and powerful nation on earth. From the very beginning they foretold it. *And what they foretold would come true.* America would rise to heights no other nation had ever known. Not that it was ever without fault or sin, but *it would aspire to fulfill its calling.*"
>
> [KAPLAN] "What calling?"
>
> [THE PROPHET] "To be a vessel of redemption, an instrument of God's purposes, a light to the world. It would give refuge to the world's poor and needy, and hope to its oppressed . . . And, as much as it fulfilled its calling or aspired to, it would become the most blessed, the most prosperous, the most powerful, and the most revered nation on the earth—*just as its founders had prophesied.*"
>
> [KAPLAN] "But there's a but coming, isn't there?"
>
> [THE PROPHET] "Yes," he replied. "There was always another side *to the covenant.* If ancient Israel fell away from God and turned against His ways, its blessings would be removed and replaced with curses."[7]

Israel was judged and fell because it failed to remain faithful to its covenant with God. She had been warned by the prophets. Using that as an example, Cahn seeks to warn Americans that this nation also faces judgment and her ultimate fall. This will happen if America repeats Israel's mistake. Repeats what mistake? That of ignoring the founders' prophecies and breaking its covenant with God. This idea, although implicit throughout *The Harbinger*, is undeniably *explicit* in places.

In chapter 19, "The Mystery Ground," Cahn significantly deepens the impression that the Founding Fathers were correct in seeing America as a new Israel. As noted earlier, Nouriel Kaplan has a dream that involves the dedication of the temple in Jerusalem under King Solomon. Then, in the middle of the dream, King Solomon mysteriously *transforms* into the first president of the United States, George Washington. The significance and troubling nature of this plot twist would be difficult to overstate. (Therefore this issue will be discussed in a separate chapter.)

Affirmation by Anglo-Israelism Proponents

In the previous section, it was suggested that the Puritans may have believed there was a direct connection between Europeans and the "ten lost tribes of Israel"—a view known as "Anglo-Israelism" (or British Israelism). Anglo-Israelism is the belief that as a result of the Assyrian invasions, the ten tribes of the Northern Kingdom of Israel were scattered, with many eventually ending up in Western Europe and particularly the British Isles.[8]

According to this belief, the British peoples are ultimately descendants of the House of Israel, while the House of Judah (the Southern Kingdom) remained in the land of Israel. In turn, America's founders, being British, were also of the House of Israel. This means that God's everlasting covenant with Abraham and his descendants remained available to the House of Israel, which was in the "*New* Israel," the United States of America. Furthermore, Old Testament prophecies to Israel remained in effect for the new nation if it would reconfirm its acceptance of God's covenant.

Anglo-Israelism has been almost uniformly rejected as unbiblical by both mainline and evangelical Christians. Yet a significant number of fringe groups and cults have incorporated this doctrine into their foundational theological positions.

The largest and best-known cult that continues to hold to Anglo-Israelism is The Church of Jesus Christ of Latter-day Saints (the Mormons). Another strong proponent of this doctrine, until after the death of its founder Herbert Armstrong in 1986, was The Worldwide Church of God.[9] But what does all of this have to do with *The Harbinger*? The answer is fairly stunning—as well as disturbing.

During his morning talk show on May 17, 2012, Glenn Beck interviewed Timothy Ballard, author of *The Covenant: America's Sacred and Immutable Connection to Ancient Israel*.[10] The topic of the interview and the thesis of Ballard's book is that America's founders, from Christopher Columbus to the Pilgrims to George Washington, established and confirmed a covenant with God and founded America based on that covenant.

As background to this interview, it is important to note that Glenn Beck converted to Mormonism in 1999.[11] Timothy Ballard received his undergraduate degree from Brigham Young University, where he graduated with honors.[12] Both hold views about America's relationship with God that are deeply rooted in their Mormon faith.

In *The Covenant*, Ballard frequently cites and quotes Herbert Armstrong to support his Anglo-Israelism position. (Armstrong was probably the single best-known non-Mormon proponent of this view.):

> The renowned Christian pastor/author, and founder of the Worldwide Church of God, Herbert Armstrong, has perhaps studied this issue as much as any other Christian writer.[13]

An underlying premise in Ballard's book is that the United States grew to be such a powerful nation because the founders had tapped into the same power that Israel had because of its covenant with God.

> [BALLARD] Why are we so powerful? What I found was that word: The covenant. The founders knew of this covenant. It's a covenant attached to the covenants of ancient Israel. They knew that power, they tapped into that power, and it worked.

A little later in the discussion, Ballard explained more specifically how this "American Covenant" began to develop, as well as its purpose—to establish a new Israel:

> [BECK] Do you have any doubt in your mind that Columbus— when he first went to Spain, he was so arrogant he didn't understand the covenant—but the second time when he went after living with the monks for a while, he was humble enough to understand the covenant and got it when he first came over.

[BALLARD] He got it. And all you have to do is look in his book of prophecies, his diary. He believed that his discovery of this new world that he thought was the Indies—he believed that this was going to create something, start a chain of events that would actually . . .

[BECK] Reestablish Israel?

[BALLARD] Exactly, exactly.

[BECK] And that's exactly the same thing that the pilgrims felt.

[BALLARD] Exactly. The pilgrims get here, they call themselves the new Israel.

The discussion continues:

[BALLARD] And Bruce's book is also complemented by another book. I don't know if you heard of a book called *The Harbinger*, by Jonathan Cahn.

[BECK] I have heard of that. I don't think I've read it.

[BALLARD] Best-selling book. Him [*sic*] and I have been talking this week. He says the same thing. He's also—he's a messianic Jew, runs the Jerusalem Center, he has a ministry. Unbelievable book. Says the exact same thing that I'm saying. The covenant has been extended from Israel, from ancient Israel to America.

[BECK] If you look at the ark [*sic*] of history, there had to be a plan to restore Israel, and it's my contention that we were that piece. We were that plan. We've done it. Now the question is, we've done our job. Are we done as a nation?

Twelve days after this interview, on May 29, and after having read *The Harbinger*, Beck discussed the book on his radio program. His understanding of what Cahn is saying is identical to Ballard's—a foundational concept in *The Harbinger* is that an American covenant with God exists:

My first impression is [that *The Harbinger* is] absolutely right. But I haven't done my homework on it. I think it could be

misread as, you know, "God's punishing America." No, no—
that's not what he's saying. He's saying that we've made a covenant
and we've broken it—and God's trying to wake us up.[14]

On his GBTV television program, Beck said the following about *The
Harbinger*:

> I find this truly amazing because this [*The Harbinger*] is making
> the case that I've been making on this program for a while—that
> we made a covenant. . . . George Washington made that cov-
> enant in a church that's right across the street from the World
> Trade Center. . . . I believe that church had God's protection
> on it to send us a message: "Do you remember that 'Church of
> Hope?'" He was sending us a message. God always returns to
> the scene of the covenant. . . .[15]

This led to Glenn Beck inviting Jonathan Cahn to personally appear
on his television program on June 26 and 27 for a two-part series. As one
would expect, the issue of a covenant between God and America comes
up—and Cahn clearly confirms his alignment with Beck's views about this:

> [BECK AT 7:49 MARK] What is important to me is the point
> you make in the book is not just about Isaiah. What you say
> is, "Ancient Israel made a covenant with God. And God will
> always remind people of the covenant and say, 'Help Me help
> you—at the place of the covenant.'"

> [CAHN] Yes.[16]

At this point, Beck is talking about the covenant between Israel and
God and the significance of the place where the covenant was made. In
the next part of the exchange, Beck sets Cahn up to make the connection
between the covenant ground of ancient Israel and the covenant ground
in the United States. There can be no doubt where Beck is going with this:

> [BECK] Tell me about this Trinity Church.

> [CAHN] Okay. There's a principle in the Bible, one of the mys-
> teries in *The Harbinger*, called the "mystery ground." What it
> is, is that when calamity comes—and this shaking comes, it
> returns to the ground where the nation was dedicated to God.

And in Israel it was the Temple Mount—that's where Solomon dedicated Israel. The calamity returns—God is saying "Wake up!" [unintelligible] "Return to where you've fallen from."[17]

Then Cahn makes exactly the connection with America that Beck is expecting:

> [CAHN] With America, what would go with that? And the thing is there is in American history—there's a foundational day. It was the first day America existed as a fully formed nation. . . . when Washington is inaugurated he gives a prophetic warning which actually says what's going to happen if America turns away from God—and it's actually coming true now. Then the government, the entire government goes on foot to dedicate America to God—the administration, the future. They go to a place—and so if we can find out what that place is we got [sic] a mystery here—that's it. And where do they do it? Well, the first capital people think is Washington. It was New York City, as we said. It was downtown Manhattan. It was—they dedicated America to God at the corner of Ground Zero. The calamity returns to the place of the dedication of the nation to God—and that's where the harbingers appeared.

Beck used the word "covenant," and his viewers would have completely understood that he was talking about the covenant. Although it is true that Cahn uses the word "dedication" instead, anyone (except perhaps someone who has read Cahn's denials of believing in an American covenant) would have understood that both Cahn and Beck were talking about exactly the same thing—two parallel nations, two parallel places of dedication, two parallel places of destruction, and two parallel covenants. There is no other way that this can be interpreted from what is said in this interview.

Cahn had the perfect opportunity to clarify that he does not actually see it as a covenant with America. Rather than doing that, Cahn tracks with Beck throughout the conversation. All he would have had to say was, "I just want to be clear, though—I don't see America's dedication as being the same as the covenant that Israel had." But Beck does see them as the same, so it is understandable why it would have been difficult for Cahn to do this.

Nor was this the only such missed opportunity to clarify Beck's misunderstanding that America is in covenant with God. As can be seen in the exchange that follows, he allowed the viewers to think that he agreed with Beck's view of an American covenant:

> [BECK] God is saying, "Hey, guys! Knock it off!" He's withdrawing His protection.
>
> (*Cahn nods affirmatively*)
>
> [BECK] He's not punishing.
>
> [CAHN] Yes. Yes.
>
> [BECK] He's withdrawing His protection because He has to.
>
> (*Cahn strongly nods affirmatively*)
>
> (*Camera cuts tighter in on Beck, with Cahn off-camera*)
>
> [BECK] Because they made a covenant and they're in violation of the covenant. Right? And they think exactly what we did after 9/11 . . .
>
> (*Cahn begins to nod affirmatively again during the last phrase*)
>
> [BECK] . . . because I was one of them. I said, "I want that . . ."
>
> [CAHN] Yes. Yes.
>
> [BECK] . . . to be one story taller. Ten stories taller.
>
> [CAHN] Right.[18]

To be fair, Cahn did not *verbally* reply to Beck's assertion, and because the camera cut was tight in on Beck at that moment, Cahn's physical reaction couldn't be seen—even though he had been nodding affirmatively with everything Beck was saying up to that point. At best, both exchanges have the appearance of being purposely ambiguous. At worst, they are misleading for the viewer if Cahn really does not believe in an American covenant—because he knows that Beck does.

This problem is compounded by the fact that at the time of his appearance on Glenn Beck's program, Cahn had already responded to some who have been critical of *The Harbinger* for multiple reasons. In these responses, Cahn emphasizes that he is not saying that God is in covenant with America. For this reason, it would have been even more important to bring this up with Beck. His decision not to do so doesn't add credibility to his denials when combined with everything else.

In his "Open Letter to T. A. McMahon of The Berean Call," Cahn writes the following:

> What it does state, is something quite different, namely, that America's founders established the nation after the pattern of ancient Israel, did dedicate it to God, and believed that in this, they were in covenant with God. Whether or not and to what degree God could honor such a commitment or prayer is left an open question. To dogmatically say that He could not honor such a prayer or dedication would exceed scriptural parameters. . . . America has been blessed. But the idea that this necessitates such a covenant, or that God entered into such a covenant, is never claimed anywhere in the book.[19]

In this response, Cahn does not definitively assert that God is in covenant with America, but he does say that he cannot be certain that such a covenant does not exist. (In fact, it is a biblical certainty that such a covenant does not exist.) This explains why Cahn can appear to be saying one thing at one time and something different at other times.

The pattern that seems to emerge is that when challenged, Cahn denies holding to an American covenant, yet he is either ambiguous or tacitly affirms such a covenant in other contexts. At best, this inconsistency and mixed message is what allows Mormons to look to *The Harbinger* for support of Anglo-Israelism.

Beck and Ballard are not the only Latter-day Saints to cite *The Harbinger* for support. On June 23, The Foundation for Indigenous Research and Mormonism (FIRM Foundation) held a conference titled, "America: The Land of Promise—God's Covenant and the Book of Mormon." The speakers included Tim Ballard and Amberli Nelson. Her short bio for the conference reads: "Researcher, Historian, Presenter of Ancient Sacred Jewish Symbology and Marriage Customs, and *The*

Harbinger book by Rabbi Jonathan Cahn."

Nelson was also a speaker on March 30 at the "Spring 2012 National Book of Mormon Evidence Conference." Her bio on that website notes:

> Sister Nelson has, for the last decade, been researching Jewish religious customs and symbology. She has found compelling new evidence that the ancient Hopewell Mound Builders may have been living the laws of Moses based on archaeological findings of the essential materials required for obedience to those laws.[20]

The unfortunate result of all this is that at least three high-profile Mormons believe that Jonathan Cahn has made a compelling case for God's covenant with ancient Israel being directly connected to America. Given Nelson's work with Jewish customs and symbology, Cahn's title of "messianic rabbi" would likely be additional credibility as a "presenter of *The Harbinger*."

Whatever may be true about Cahn's actual views concerning an American covenant, such use of *The Harbinger* to support the uniquely cultic view of Anglo-Israelism presents the author with a serious problem. The significance of this can be seen in the following illustration of the situation.

What if an evangelical had written an article or book about the Lord Jesus Christ such that Mormon theologians began to appeal to it specifically for support of an important point in their heretical Christology? This would be a disastrous development.

If the author had been misunderstood, he would be obligated to clear this up as soon as possible. He would need to remove or reword the problem statements so that Mormons could not use them in this way. This wouldn't be difficult to accomplish, but it would require pulling current copies from the market and the printing of a second edition. It would also require a public acknowledgment of the problem with the way he had chosen to express his views.

What would not be sufficient would be for the author to simply make a few public statements to attempt to clarify his views and leave it at that while the original editions of the book remained on the market. Neither would it be sufficient to begin trying to publicly engage those who were using his work to support their false views about Christ. The problem would be further compounded if, during interviews, the author made ambiguous statements that confused the situation even more. This perfectly illustrates a major flaw of *The Harbinger*.

None of this is to remotely suggest that Cahn holds to Anglo-Israelism. And, in fact, it would be difficult to imagine that he does not firmly oppose this view. However, Bible believers should be much more cautious and discerning than some have been in their acceptance and promotion of *The Harbinger* in its present form for the following reasons:

1. Anglo-Israelism and an American covenant view are often inseparable.

2. *The Harbinger* presents an American covenant view clearly enough for Anglo-Israelism proponents to embrace the book and appeal to it for support of that view.

3. Anglo-Israelism has been almost exclusively a defining characteristic of certain cults such as Mormons and the Worldwide Church of God.

4. Although Cahn has denied holding to an American covenant view in some contexts, he has tacitly affirmed this view, or remained non-committal, or been ambiguous at the very least in other contexts.

5. A growing number of conservative evangelical theologians also interpret Cahn's words as clearly promoting an American covenant view.

NOT ISRAEL, BUT ASSYRIA

The Scriptures clearly mitigate against the idea that America or any other nation besides Israel would or could be in a covenant relationship with God. It was God, not Abraham, who initiated the unique, everlasting, and unconditional Abrahamic Covenant with Israel. There is no scriptural indication that any Gentile nation can initiate a covenant with God. (Cahn acknowledged this in the April 4 discussion.)

The promises of the Abrahamic Covenant specifically include *the land*. Apart from Israel's presence in the land, there is no fulfillment. Therefore, the physical descendants of Abraham, Isaac, and Jacob[21] must be in the land to inherit the covenant promises. This is one reason why the return of Jewish people to the land of Israel since 1948 has been so significant.

In other words, even if one entertains the idea of Anglo-Israelism just for the sake of argument, America cannot be the location of fulfillment. America cannot be a new Israel geographically. The extent of the geographical boundaries of the promised land is very specific and must be understood literally. To do otherwise is to spiritualize God's promises and turn the historical text into an allegory.

America's founders were therefore biblically wrong on several counts. Those founders who may have held even an early form of Anglo-Israelism were wrong. Those who held an American Covenant view were wrong. Even though they may have sought to establish a covenant with God, there is no scriptural basis for concluding that God actually accepted and entered into such a covenant with America. *America is not parallel to Israel in any way.*

If America were parallel to any nation it might be to Assyria rather than to Israel. Interestingly, in *The Harbinger,* Cahn does present Nineveh as an example of what happens when there is a major spiritual shift within a culture.[22] Untold numbers in Nineveh repented and turned to God under the preaching of the prophet Jonah.[23] This is therefore a good example to use when calling a people to repentance—and Cahn has this part right.

Furthermore, there is no inherent problem in suggesting that when many individuals are in a right relationship with God, the collective result could be an abundance of blessings experienced at the national level. Assyria may well have experienced God's favor as long as the people in her capital continued to faithfully live out their personal relationship with Him. At the very least their repentance certainly forestalled God's judgment of Nineveh.

However, this is far different from suggesting that Assyria was in a relationship with God as a *nation.* This is not just a matter of mere semantics. Even though Cahn's intention was not to write a theological dissertation, by choosing to incorporate the concept of covenants into his story, the burden falls on him to deal with this highly theological subject in a biblical manner.

Although Nineveh is a biblical example of the collective results of the repentance of individuals, there is no scriptural evidence that suggests that Nineveh was ever in a special covenant relationship with God at the national (or city) level. Therefore, God's dealings with Assyria as a Gentile nation cannot be equated to His dealings with Israel as His chosen nation. Likewise, although God's dealings with Assyria and America as Gentile nations can be legitimately equated, His dealings with America cannot be equated to His dealings with Israel.

WHERE IS NATIONAL ISRAEL?

The Harbinger does not explicitly state that God has permanently rejected national Israel. But a troubling fact is that Cahn does not mention either *modern-day* or *future* Israel at all. This is significant, because the sense that one gets from reading the book is that as a result of Israel's failure to heed the prophets' warnings it was permanently annihilated. *The Harbinger* leaves ancient Israel lying in ruins and then jumps forward to twenty-first century America, which does not include the whole story—a very important part of the story, in the context of judgment. It would be difficult to overstate just how serious this issue is.

One significant problem is that the author fails to mention any of God's unconditional promises to Israel concerning the land, descendants, and blessings.[24] Perhaps he didn't have to directly incorporate them into *The Harbinger*'s storyline, but because of the many biblical promises that speak of Israel's assured future restoration after judgment, this becomes critical if Israel's history is being repeated in America, as Cahn believes.

If Israel's future restoration by God is certain, is this also true of America? Conversely, if Israel has permanently forfeited her chance of future restoration, does this mean that America may also be facing permanent destruction? Cahn's failure to mention modern and future Israel gives the distinct impression that her destruction was final. Although this omission may add to the dramatic effect of *The Harbinger*, it is also thoroughly unbiblical and misleading.

The corollary to the message of judgment in *The Harbinger* is that America can avert God's wrath through repentance and a return to Him. However, the many Old Testament passages that speak of Israel's future restoration are ignored in favor of the single example of Nineveh, which speaks only of *postponed* judgment—not the possibility of restoration after judgment.

Would that have taken the alarmist edge off the book? Is Israel's God-given claim to the Promised Land too much of a political "hot potato" in today's era of political correctness? Why would a messianic rabbi fail to make at least some reference to Israel's coming restoration? The most important question, however, is: How does one justify omitting one of the most important themes related to Israel's judgment in the entire Word of God?

This problem is further compounded by Cahn's failure to mention Isaiah 9:1-7. It is impossible to correctly understand Isaiah 9:8-11 apart from the preceding verses—particularly verses 6 and 7 about the coming of the Messiah who will rule over the nations—from Israel.

Isaiah 9:6-7—

> For unto us a Child is born, Unto us a Son is given; And the government will be upon His shoulder. And His name will be called Wonderful, Counselor, Mighty God, Everlasting Father, Prince of Peace. Of the increase of His government and peace There will be no end, Upon the throne of David and over His kingdom, to order it and establish it with judgment and justice From that time forward, even forever. The zeal of the LORD of hosts will perform this.

Granted, it is beyond the scope of *The Harbinger* to include a fully developed eschatology or end-times scenario. However, the only thing that one can learn from the book is that ancient Israel did not repent and was destroyed. This is where Cahn leaves it.

[THE PROPHET] "So what happens if a warning is given, if the alarms go off, and nobody listens?"

[KAPLAN] "Then it happens."

[THE PROPHET] "So then it happens."

[KAPLAN] "But does it have to happen?" I asked.

[THE PROPHET] "If the warning is rejected, then, yes, it has to happen."

[KAPLAN] "But people can change, and a nation can alter its course."

[THE PROPHET] "Yes. That's the hope. That's the purpose of a warning. A changed course means a changed end. But an unchanged course means an unchanged end. Then it has to happen."

[KAPLAN] "As it did to ancient Israel?"

Once again, this gives the distinct impression that Israel met its final end, which is precisely Cahn's warning to America: If America does not turn to God soon, it will mean the end of the nation. If Cahn does believe that Israel still has a future, it is unfortunate that he invoked America's founders with their belief in a new Israel, while speaking only of ancient Israel's destruction and nothing of her future restoration.

America's early founders believed that as a group—as a new nation—they represented Christ's kingdom. No longer under the established church in Europe, they were now free as the *true church* to establish God's kingdom upon the earth—beginning with America as the "New Israel." In their view, this was their God-given right and responsibility. As a result, there is little practical difference between their view of America as God's covenant people and replacement theology, which sees the church as God's covenant people—with no place left for national Israel.

This highlights the problem of lifting a passage from its context. Although Cahn has said that he rejects and in fact teaches directly against replacement theology, *The Harbinger* nonetheless has strong overtones of that very doctrine. And because it involves America as a nation, this could well play into the hands of those who wrongly believe it is the church's responsibility to establish God's kingdom on the earth in preparation for Christ's return. Just as proponents of Anglo-Israelism believe that they have found a new supporting resource in *The Harbinger*, so too proponents of "kingdom now" theology, reconstructionism, and dominionism could have another weapon in their arsenal.

CHAPTER 9

MISSING CRITICAL ELEMENTS

CHRIST, THE CHURCH, CHRISTIANS: WHERE ARE THEY?

FROM THE COMING of the Holy Spirit on the day of Pentecost (Acts 2) to the present day, building the church of Jesus Christ has been the central focus of what God is doing in the world. Made up of born-again believers in Christ (Christians), the church has been entrusted with the gospel and commissioned to proclaim the good news of forgiven sin and eternal life—the message of salvation through faith in Christ. God works in and through the church to call unbelieving sinners to faith in Christ. The Father draws the lost to the Son through the Holy Spirit.

Cahn's omission of present or future Israel from the book is surprising, but his failure to mention the church is startling. The word "church" is never used except in reference to a building.

But there is more.

Cahn does not include the word "Christian" in the book either.

And yet more.

The author does not use the word "Christ." ("Messiah" is used—but only twice).[1]

Nor does he mention Christ's second coming or the kingdom that Christ will establish.

MISSING CRITICAL ELEMENTS

This is not to say that Jesus is not referenced or mentioned anywhere in the book. Cahn does devote chapter 21, "Eternity," to extensively discussing salvation and does refer to Jesus—which is very positive in principle (and will be discussed later). However, except for chapter 21, Jesus is only referred to one other time in one paragraph on one page (p. 118). And even in chapter 21, the name "Jesus" is used a total of two times. He is referred to more times than that in the chapter but not by name.

Of course any author would have to make these literary decisions and decide on the right balance. Yet Cahn's choices seem to be extremely out of balance given the ultimate purpose of *The Harbinger*.

In the context of a book that is supposed to be calling a nation to repentance to avoid God's judgment, such omissions are not only disconcerting and inexplicable—they are unbiblical. The New Testament makes it clear that every future judgment of God involves Jesus Christ, yet Cahn never makes that association. Every future judgment of God is in the context of Christ's second coming, yet Cahn never mentions His return. And every future judgment of God is preparatory to the establishment of Christ's kingdom, yet Cahn never tells the reader where this is all heading.

One almost senses that Cahn has explicitly avoided saying too much about Christ and Christians and Christianity. Trying to avoid giving the impression that this is only about religion is a good thing. But leaving out so much crucial biblical truth concerning the nature of the coming judgment is just wrong.

ACTUAL PROPHESIED EVENTS: WHERE ARE THEY?

The omission of this and other important issues directly associated with God's coming judgments is troubling. An abundance of biblical material could have been used to warn in explicit detail of what is really coming.

Just a few examples include the Rapture of the church in 1 Thessalonians chapter 4, the rise of Antichrist in 2 Thessalonians chapter 2, the seven years of tribulation judgments culminating with the return of Christ in Revelation chapters 4 through 19.

Those prophecies, being directly connected with the coming judgment, are powerful yet none of these events are mentioned in *The Harbinger*.

-75-

In addition, a whole array of current events could have been legitimately incorporated into the story, setting the stage for genuine fulfillment of the prophetic Scriptures (as opposed to the manufactured fulfillment in *The Harbinger*).

Why were these not mentioned? Perhaps in Cahn's mind they would not naturally fit into the storyline. Perhaps he did not think there was room in the narrative—and of course one of the most difficult aspects of anything like this is not just determining what to write but what to leave out.

Whatever the reason, the inescapable fact is that Cahn's theories about Isaiah 9:10 cannot be reconciled and correlated with other relevant biblical prophecies—which are completely ignored. The result is that genuine biblical exegesis has been sacrificed on the altar of speculation.

JEWS, ISRAEL, MUSLIMS, ISLAM: WHERE ARE THEY?

As has been noted, modern-day Israel is not mentioned. Future Israel and her coming restoration are not mentioned. The church is not mentioned. Christ's return and His kingdom—not mentioned. Christians are not mentioned by name. Present-day Jews are mentioned only once in passing.[2]

Since Cahn does not shy away from discussing the "War on Terror," how odd that neither Muslims nor Islam are mentioned anywhere in the book. He does directly discuss al Qaeda but only in the context of the wars in Iraq and Afghanistan. That wouldn't be a problem if it weren't for the fact that he makes it sound as if the War on Terror is a war between nations as it was between Assyria and Israel. It is not.

It's a war that transcends national and ethnic boundaries. It is driven by an ideology—by the religion and religious convictions of those who started this war on 9/11. This is not just a War on Terror. This is a war against *Islamic Jihadists* who have chosen terrorism as their preferred and primary tactic. This is a war against those who are prepared to kill themselves and as many infidels as they can because of their belief that their God-given mission is to establish a worldwide Islamic Caliphate.

Shiite Muslims believe this caliphate will be established after the reappearance of the Twelfth Imam, the Mahdi—the Islamic messiah—whom Allah has hidden and kept alive for over a millennium.[3] Some among these Shia believe, as does Mahmoud Ahmadinejad, the president of Iran, that the Imam's appearance can be hastened by destabilizing the world through creating international turmoil and chaos—especially involving military conflict.[4]

This clearly has the marks of being a major contributing factor in a worldwide end-times scenario, which includes far more than just God's judgment against the United States. If these are setting the stage, then three major prophesied biblical events could quickly come into play:

1. The Rapture of the church, when all Christians, living and dead, will be caught up to meet the Lord Jesus Christ in the clouds.[5]

2. The seven-year period of tribulation, the final week of Daniel's prophesied seventy weeks,[6] when God's judgments will be unleashed against the kingdoms of this world, Antichrist, and Satan himself.[7]

3. The return of Jesus Christ to the earth to establish His 1,000-year reign from the throne of David in Jerusalem.[8]

Even though there might be some difference between Cahn's views and those of this author on the relative timing of the Rapture and the beginning of the Tribulation, Cahn has stated that he essentially agrees with all three of the above points.[9] He therefore fully understands that these events and any judgment in the near future are inseparably linked. The urgency of the hour in calling for repentance is because of what the Bible clearly says is coming—not because of an imagined link between Isaiah 9:10 and America.

Of course, the author of a fictional book has the freedom and prerogative to take his story in any direction he wants as he develops his plot. But again, the problem is that this fictional story is only a framework for telling what Cahn believes is the *real* story.

Unfortunately, he has left out what is perhaps the most significant part of that real story. He could have used any number of potential storylines to present solid biblical truth, both historical and prophetic, and then genuinely matched this up with clear and unambiguous historical facts and current events to craft a thoroughly accurate and compelling Christian fictional novel. Cahn's failure to do so only adds to the confusion about biblical prophecy and future events that already plagues so many people.

On Amazon.com, the comments of the readers who gave *The Harbinger* a five-star rating indicate that many of them believe they now have a much better understanding of both biblical prophecy, current events, and the relationship between the two. Sadly they do not. The only things they now understand are the unbiblical interpretations and speculative theories of Jonathan Cahn. The scope of this tragedy is underscored by the fact that *The Harbinger* has ranked second or third in sales in Amazon.com's theology category for months.

CHAPTER 10

THE ANCIENT MYSTERY: THE NINE HARBINGERS

AS PREVIOUSLY NOTED, the fictional part of the story centers around a "mystery" connected with nine small, engraved clay discs that date from "the sixth or seventh century B.C. in the kingdom of Judah."[1] There is also a tenth seal that was sent to Kaplan by The Prophet prior to their initial encounter. This is Kaplan's personal seal, which has been given to mark him as a "watchman on the wall" who is to sound the alarm and call America to repentance before God's final judgment is unleashed against her.

In the story, the original purpose of the nine seals was to warn the Northern Kingdom of Israel of progressive stages in God's judgment as prophesied in Isaiah 9:10:

> *The bricks have fallen down,*
> *But we will rebuild with hewn stones;*
> *The sycamores have been cut down,*
> *But we will replace them with cedars.*

As such, the nine seals were "harbingers" of impending events that would take place if Israel did not heed them as warnings—events that would ultimately lead to a catastrophic final judgment resulting in Israel's total destruction and collapse. As noted earlier, although the nine seals are only part of the fictional narrative, they do represent nine actual "harbingers," or signs, that Cahn believes he has identified in the Isaiah passage. Beyond this, he also believes that in identifying these harbingers he has discovered an ancient mystery—a pattern of judgment represented by these signs—which is appearing once again in the United States of America. This is what the author means when he writes, "what is contained within the story is real."

The First Harbinger: The Breach

Fact concerning Israel: God removed His hedge of protection from Israel, which allowed the Assyrians to attack the nation.

Claim concerning America: God removed His hedge of protection from the United States, which allowed the terrorists to attack on 9/11.

Although God protects whomever, whenever, and however He chooses, His "hedge of protection" specifically prevents external harm from befalling the object of His care. Such protection is mentioned only twice in the Old Testament—once in Satan's accusation against God concerning Job (Job 1:10) and once concerning the nation of Israel (Isaiah 5:5). In the New Testament, it appears in only one parable, which is also about Israel (Matthew 21:33; Mark 12:1). There is no indication anywhere in Scripture that any other nation ever has or ever will be protected in this particular way.

If the Scriptures never connect a hedge of protection with any nation except Israel, which was completely unique, how can it be claimed with any certainty that 9/11 marked the *removal* of such protection from America? Such a conclusion is purely speculative.

Furthermore, even if God had provided such a hedge of protection around America, is it not possible to also argue that it is still in place? There has not been another successful terrorist attack on American soil since September 11, 2001—even though U.S. intelligence has frequently indicated that the motivation, intent, and plotting to launch more attacks has continued unabated.

A recent Reuters article reported that "law enforcement and homeland security personnel face an average of fifty-five daily encounters with 'known or suspected terrorists.'"[2] That is over 20,000 per year. So on what basis does someone suggest that God has removed His hedge of protection—if such a thing even exists for any nation but Israel? Or would Cahn now need to say that God has put the hedge back into place? Cahn's theory aligns with neither the biblical evidence nor with the contemporary evidence of current events.

What about all those countries in Europe that have not experienced any attacks on their soil for more than sixty years? What about Canada? Does this mean that a similar hedge of protection remains in place around those nations? It is fairly clear that Cahn has developed a specious argument.

If America enjoyed God's hedge of protection until 9/11, then what about Pearl Harbor? A common objection to this question is that Hawaii was not on American soil. However, that is an uninformed view. Hawaii was an American territory, and therefore the attack was against America and on American soil.

The year following that attack, the Japanese captured and occupied two Aleutian islands of the Alaska territory. The United States purchased Alaska from Russia in 1867[3]—it was U.S. soil.

The British captured Detroit on August 16th during the War of 1812.[4] Later in the war, Washington D.C. was captured and burned to the ground.[5]

In addition to those wars, terrorist attacks were carried out in the United States prior to 9/11:

- In 1920, a TNT bomb on Wall Street killed 35 people. Though the crime was never solved, it was believed to be the work of Bolshevist and anarchist terrorists.[6]

- In 1975, a Puerto Rican nationalist group claimed responsibility for a bomb in New York City that killed four and injured more than fifty people.[7]

- In 1993, the World Trade Center was bombed by foreign nationals (Al Qaeda was suspected) with the intent of taking down both towers. This attack killed six and injured over 1000.[8]

If God's hedge of protection was removed, allowing the terrorist attacks in 2001, when was it put back into place? Was this hedge of protection also absent when the other military and terrorist attacks took place on American soil? At which points in history was the hedge of protection *in* place—and when was it *not*? Given the lack of successful attacks over the past decade, should it be assumed that God's hedge of protection has now been put *back* in place?

It quickly becomes clear that any event could be interpreted in any number of ways when the literary context doesn't provide the exclusive framework for interpretation. It is this method of handling the biblical text that so frequently exposes Christians to the challenge of the well-worn cliché, "Well, that's just your interpretation." This charge is easily leveled against *The Harbinger* because of the break with the text and context.

Of course, all of the above could be dismissed as simply malicious nit-picking of unimportant details in order to tear down *The Harbinger*—and, in the process, "missing the forest for the trees." Unfortunately, it is Cahn who has forced this minute analysis by making sweeping claims while overwhelming his readers with tedious technical details. Since he has built his case on such details, they are not only fair game but they *must* be examined. To do otherwise is to give an author carte blanche to make any claim without accountability. Allowing this to go unchallenged would be irresponsible. Furthermore, if Cahn *is* trading in facts and truth, a closer examination would ultimately do nothing but prove him to be right.

Second Harbinger: The Terrorist

Fact concerning Israel: The Assyrians who attacked the Northern Kingdom of Israel employed some tactics that would today be labeled terrorism.

Claim concerning America: Multiple direct links between the 9/11 al Qaeda terrorists and the ancient Assyrians demonstrate that the historic fulfillment of Isaiah 9:10 is repeating itself.

In order to bolster the idea of a connection between ancient Israel and America, Cahn goes out of his way to demonstrate that the Assyrians of the eighth century B.C. were terrorists and were linked to the 9/11 terrorist attacks.

> [Kaplan] "The Assyrians were terrorists?" I asked.
>
> [The Prophet] "As much as any people have ever been. Terrorism is defined as: the systematic application of terror, violence, and intimidation to achieve a specific end. Terror as an applied science—*this was the dark gift the Assyrians gave to the world.*"[9]

The Assyrians gave terrorism to the world? Had no one prior to the Assyrians effectively utilized what would today be called "terrorist tactics?" What about the many nations that continually harassed and attacked Israel—including the Moabites, the Ammonites, the Canaanites, the Philistines, the Egyptians, and the Edomites? This entire section has the feeling of just trying too hard.

Where does it end?

Beyond this, on what basis is the parallel between Israel and America limited to just Isaiah 9:10 and the Assyrians? What about the countless other prophecies concerning Israel in relation to her other enemies? Why couldn't some, most, or even all of these prophecies represent a pattern of God's judgment that could be related to the United States? If even one is thought to be applicable to America—independent of the text—on what basis could others be discounted? When will the next author write the next best-selling book about another prophecy using the same methods as Cahn? Once the anchor rope to the Word of God has been cut, the drift away from objective interpretation is inevitable.

The link that isn't

Another part of the second harbinger discussion that also conveys the idea of trying too hard is the attempt to "connect the dots" between the ancient Assyrians, and their modern-day counterparts.

[KAPLAN] "Assyria is Iraq?"

[THE PROPHET] "It's the same land."

[KAPLAN] "The nation under judgment . . . is drawn into conflict with the land of Assyria . . . ancient Israel . . . now America."

[THE PROPHET] "And American troops were now walking the same earth on which the feet of Assyrian soldiers had once marched. And among those watching them pass by were those who could still claim to be the descendants of the ancient Assyrians."

[KAPLAN] "Their actual flesh-and-blood descendants?" I asked.

[THE PROPHET] "Yes," he replied. "And who knows but that the veins of the 9/11 terrorists did not also flow with the blood of the ancient Assyrians?"

[KAPLAN] "So ancient Israel, in its time of judgment, was drawn into war with Assyria, which is now Iraq."

[THE PROPHET] "Yes," he answered.

[KAPLAN] "And now America was drawn into a war with the land of Assyria—Iraq."

Interestingly, Cahn tries to tie this all together with a question rather than a statement when The Prophet asks, "And who knows but that the veins of the 9/11 terrorists . . . ?" Clearly he is making a statement, albeit in such a way that it's somewhat difficult to hold him accountable for it. But trying to put Assyrian blood into the 9/11 terrorists is a detail that arguably would have been better left out of the narrative because it is yet another chink in his armor.

It has generally been acknowledged that Saddam Hussein and Iraq were not connected in any way to the 9/11 attacks despite early theories to the contrary. Rather than being attacked by a particular nation, as was ancient Israel, the 9/11 operation was al Qaeda's, which is not directly connected to any country. This represents the first of several points where this part of his theory falls apart.

Al Qaeda was not based in Iraq but in Afghanistan, which is not historically connected to ancient Assyria. Other countries that are connected to al Qaeda include Pakistan, Sudan, and tangentially Saudi Arabia, because fifteen of the nineteen hijackers carried Saudi passports. (The only reason that the mastermind behind the plot, Osama bin Laden, did not carry a Saudi passport is because his citizenship had been revoked when he was overseeing and funding the development of al Qaeda from inside Sudan.[10]) However, Saudi Arabia is located south of the extent of what had been the ancient Assyrian empire throughout most or all of its history. Furthermore, Saudi Arabia is not even listed among twenty-six countries with any appreciable Assyrian population.[11] Each of these facts further disconnects the ancient Assyrians from the 9/11 attackers.

Although Assyria is no longer an empire or even a nation, Assyrians do form a specific ethnic group—of which 95 percent identify themselves as Christians, not Muslims.[12] According to Assyrian history, this region was reached by the apostles Thomas, Bartholomew, and Thaddeus shortly after Christ's death.[13]

The following two quotes are from the home page of *Nineveh.com*, which is identified as *"the home of the indigenous Aramaic-speaking Christian Assyrians."* (The first quote is in reference to the 9/11 terrorist attacks.):

> On behalf of the Assyrians living in the United State[s] and throughout the world, we extend our thoughts and condolences to the families of the victims and to the American nation during the tragic acts of barbaric terrorism inflicted towards all of humanity.[14]

* * *

> The Assyrians of today are the indigenous Aramaic-speaking descendants of the ancient Assyrian people, one of the earliest civilizations emerging in the Middle East, and have a history spanning over 6750 years. Assyrians are not Arabian, we are not Kurdish, our religion is not Islam. The Assyrians are Christian, with our own unique language, culture and heritage. Although the Assyrian empire ended in 612 B.C., history is replete with recorded details of the continuous presence of the Assyrian people till the present time.[15]

The lengths to which Cahn goes to establish links involving unnecessary minutiae tends to get tedious after a while and actually contributes to his undoing more than once. One very tenuous link is when he tries to establish another literal prophetic fulfillment based on a proposed connection between the Akkadian spoken by the ancient Assyrians and modern-day Arabic:

[KAPLAN] "So the Assyrians are the spiritual fathers of al Qaeda."

[THE PROPHET] "Yes, and not only the spiritual," he replied.

[KAPLAN] "And what does that mean?"

[THE PROPHET] "The Assyrians were children of the Middle East, so too the terrorists of 9/11. The Assyrians were a Semitic people, so too the terrorists. The Assyrians spoke a language called Akkadian. The tongue is long extinct, but there is still spoken in the modern world one language considered to be the closest of all tongues to ancient Akkadian."

[KAPLAN] "Which is . . . ?"

[THE PROPHET] "Arabic."

[KAPLAN] "Arabic—the tongue of al Qaeda and the 9/11 terrorists."

[THE PROPHET] "Yes, and so when the leaders of al Qaeda plotted their attack on America, and as the terrorists communicated with each other on 9/11 to carry it out, they did so using words and speech patterns that mirrored those used by the Assyrian leaders and warriors as they planned and executed their attack on Israel two and half thousand years earlier in 732 B.C."

A potential problem with the linguistic aspect of this part of Cahn's theory can be found on the *Assyrian International News Agency* website:

Assyrians have used two languages throughout their history: ancient Assyrian (Akkadian), and Modern Assyrian (neo-syriac). Akkadian was written with the cuneiform writing system, on clay tablets, and was in use from the beginning to about 750 BC. By 750 BC, a new way of writing, on parchment, leather, or papyrus, was developed, and the people who brought this method of writing with them, the Arameans, would eventually see their language, Aramaic, supplant Ancient Assyrian because of the technological breakthrough in writing. Aramaic was made the second official language of the Assyrian empire in 752 BC.[16]

Assyria's attacks on Israel occurred years after the transition to Aramaic was well under way. Of course, Akkadian was still being spoken and even incorporated into the localized Aramaic, but the evidence continues to mount that Cahn overreaches—and grasps at some very thin straws to overwhelm and persuade his readers with the sheer number of these things that supposedly cannot be mere coincidences. It's almost like watching a great illusionist. What the audience thinks it sees is truly astounding—but it isn't real, with the performer relying entirely on misdirection for the illusion to work.

Even the issue of the Assyrians being "children of the Middle East" and a Semitic people is an empty argument. The exact same thing is true of all the descendants of Abraham just as it is of the Jewish people of today. It is curious that Cahn would attempt to use this for support even in a passing comment, as it only serves to further undermine his own theory.

The bottom line is that the 9/11 terrorists were not Assyrians, they were not Christians,[17] they did not speak Aramaic or a derivative, and the proposed ancient Assyrian–9/11 terrorist link almost certainly does not exist. It too is fabricated from almost nothing.

THIRD HARBINGER: THE FALLEN BRICKS

FACT CONCERNING ISRAEL: Clay bricks were originally used as the primary building material for the city walls, houses, and most other structures.

CLAIM CONCERNING AMERICA: Bricks fell from buildings when the World Trade Center towers collapsed.

This is arguably another example of how the author stretches things too far to find support for his theory that the harbingers have been manifested in America. In the historical context, because so much was built with bricks, "the bricks have fallen" would indicate widespread destruction throughout the Northern Kingdom—the city walls, the buildings, the houses, virtually everything.

In both *The Harbinger* and the documentary, *The Isaiah 9:10 Judgment*, Cahn emphasizes that the significance is that the buildings fell—and this forms the parallel to the destruction at the hands of the Assyrians. However, as tragic as it was, only a relatively few buildings fell on 9/11—not an entire city, let alone an entire nation. And although there had been an airport security breach, this was not a breach of America's military defenses, even when the attack on the Pentagon is considered. The breach in America that led to the fallen bricks is nothing like what happened to ancient Israel.

The pattern of forcing current events into the Isaiah 9:10 prophecy continues with the author's discussion of the bricks themselves:

[THE PROPHET] "The American towers fell with the same sudden-ness as did the clay bricks and buildings of ancient Israel. In a matter of moments, they had become a heap of ruins. And yet the connection was still more literal."

[KAPLAN] "What do you mean?"

[THE PROPHET] "The ruin heap of Ground Zero was filled with steel, concrete, and glass, but not only that."

[KAPLAN] "With what?"

[THE PROPHET] "Bricks."

[KAPLAN] "As in 'The bricks have fallen.'"

[THE PROPHET] "The fallen bricks of ancient Israel comprised a warning concerning the nation's future. So too the fallen bricks of Ground Zero."[18]

The fallen bricks in ancient Israel were far more than merely a warn-ing—they were the ruins of a destroyed city. However, fallen bricks were only very incidental in the World Trade Center attacks. In fact, it has been suggested that it was *the lack* of masonry construction that allowed the col-lapse of the towers:

> On September 11, 2001, airplanes struck two 110-story office towers in New York and the Pentagon in Washington, D.C. The towers (WTC 1 and WTC 2) collapsed in less than two hours, and another building in the complex (WTC 7) collapsed later in the afternoon. *These buildings had few or no masonry components.*[19]

In contrast, a nearby brick building with a steel and concrete superstruc-ture, actually *fared better* than other buildings *because of the brick exterior*:

> Although the framing deflected as much as 2 ft into the building, the *masonry infill restrained the columns from collapse.* The steel structure was not affected. None of the damage threatened the structural integrity of the building.[20]

The 9/11 attacks were a horrific tragedy that left a deep scar on the hearts and minds of the American people. The terrorists successfully terrorized the city and the nation—so much loss in so many ways.

However, with no intent to minimize the tragedy in any way, it must be recognized that compared to the utter devastation in ancient Israel, there was relatively little destruction in New York City. The small number of bricks that fell in 2001 was inconsequential—not at all comparable to what happened in the eighth century B.C.

If one is going to rely on such threadbare evidence to prove a theory with such far-reaching implications, then such superficial characteristics could be used to prove a relationship between *any* two catastrophic events. These hardly rise to the level of interesting coincidences let alone literal prophetic fulfillment. There simply is no match, no pattern, and no parallel to Isaiah 9:10.

FOURTH HARBINGER: THE TOWER

FACT CONCERNING ISRAEL: Israel's leaders demonstrated a spirit of defiance against God with their declaration that the destroyed city would be rebuilt with no thought of repentance.

CLAIM CONCERNING AMERICA: America's leaders followed exactly in the footsteps of Israel's leaders when they declared that the destroyed WTC towers would be rebuilt.

On the fourth clay seal is the image of a tower that is said to look like the Tower of Babel. With nothing in the text about a tower (more on this later), how does this fit in? In the story, it is connected with a "spirit of defiance" that prompts the declaration by ancient Israel to rebuild the leveled city with hewn stone—and in the case of the WTCs, to rebuild a tower at Ground Zero.

> [KAPLAN] "So if the ancient mystery is joined to America, then somehow 9/11 has to be linked to the words 'We will rebuild.'"

> [THE PROPHET] "Correct. In the wake of their calamity, the leaders of ancient Israel proclaimed, 'We will rebuild'—the first sign of defiance. If the mystery holds *and has now applied to America*, we would expect to hear the same vow, the same three words, in the wake of 9/11, now proclaimed by American leaders."

[KAPLAN] "And did it happen? Did they say it?"

[THE PROPHET] "Yes. They said it. Not that it wouldn't have been natural to speak of rebuilding, but the way these three words continuously came forth from the mouths of American leaders, spoken, over and over again, as public proclamations, was striking."[21]

Israel knew the Assyrian attacks were a judgment they had brought upon themselves. When they declared that they would rebuild, they were intentionally shaking their fists in defiance at both their enemies and their God.

But is this what America's leaders were doing? In both the book and the documentary by *WND*, Cahn attempts to make the case that this is *exactly* what they were doing. He contends that America's leaders were proudly and arrogantly acting in defiance of God when they spoke of rebuilding. Through The Prophet, the author cites those he says were defiant when they used the phrase, "We will rebuild":

[THE PROPHET] "From the mayor of New York City in the wake of the attack: 'We will rebuild . . .'

"From the state's senior senator: 'We will rebuild . . .'

"From the state's governor: 'We will rebuild. And we will move forward.'

"From the state's junior senator: 'We will rebuild . . .'

"From the city's mayor at the time of the rebuilding: 'We will rebuild, renew, and remain the capital of the free world.'

"From the president of the United States: 'We will rebuild New York City.'

"One way or another, each leader would end up proclaiming the same words of defiance proclaimed thousands of years before by the leaders of ancient Israel."

In the documentary, Cahn says,

[JONATHAN CAHN] "We'll rebuild New York. We'll rebuild Ground Zero. We'll rebuild better than . . ." again and again and again, without anything of repentance, that's the key. So, it becomes something of pride and of arrogance—about we're going to show the world, but we're not turning to God at all.[22]

On June 16, 2012, *WND* continued to develop this theme with an exclusive article titled "Obama 'Fulfills' Isaiah 9:10 Prophecy—Again."[23] The article dealt with the president's visit to Ground Zero on June 15, when he signed one of the steel beams at One World Trade Center with the following message: "We remember. We rebuild. We come back stronger!"

Cahn is quoted giving his prompt response to the president's words:

> "On June 14, two of the mysteries of *The Harbinger*, foreshadowed in the book came true," explained Cahn. "Obama went to Ground Zero to see the still rising tower. He was given a beam which will constitute the tower's final and highest beam. On the beam, the president wrote eight words—which were, in effect, a summation of the ancient vow of judgment: 'We Remember, We Rebuild, We Come Back Stronger!'
>
> "Now the words and the tower have been joined together in reality—and the one who did it was the president of the United States," he told *WND*. "One subtle difference in the words, is that the vow is spoken in the future tense. But now the words inscribed on the towers are in the present tense. In other words, they not only speak of the defiant vow, but of the fact that the vow is being fulfilled. This," says Cahn, "constitutes another ominous sign."

WND identifies Obama's actions as a fulfillment of prophecy. Cahn identifies them as fulfillment of a vow. Once again, both Cahn and *WND* clearly demonstrate their mutually held view that Isaiah 9:10 is a prophecy directed not only to ancient Israel but also to America. By describing the event as "fulfillment," Cahn makes it impossible to accept his consistent protest in which he says that recent events are only a parallel or pattern of what happened in the eighth century B.C.

This is all quite misleading because although standing in defiance of America's *enemies*, there is no evidence that the talk of rebuilding had anything to do with an intentional refusal to turn to God. However, since the case for defiance cannot be made based just on the words "We will rebuild," Cahn lays the groundwork for his argument through the words of The Prophet:

[THE PROPHET] "Remember, it's not just the words but the context surrounding them and the spirit behind them. The problem wasn't the rebuilding. The problem was the spirit and the motive behind the rebuilding."

Passing judgment?

So it had to do with their motives—what they meant, what was in their hearts and minds, what their intentions were. How does Cahn know what these were? Did he talk with them as he prepared to write his book? Did he ask them what they were thinking on those days? Did he ask them what they intended to convey to their respective audiences? What if it later turned out that he was wrong? That could well happen if some of these men happen to read *The Harbinger*.

It is one thing to make an observation and report what someone said. Of course they said what they said. As Cahn notes, that's a matter of public record. It's quite another thing to assign motives without specific knowledge of what someone was thinking or what was going on in someone's heart. The Bible calls that judging and warns against it in very strong terms:

Matthew 7:1–2 —

Judge not, that you be not judged. For with what judgment you judge, you will be judged; and with the measure you use, it will be measured back to you.

There is a place for passing a righteous judgment, but this was not that place.

Inconsistent logic

Cahn ends up contradicting himself concerning the intentions of these men. Here he argues that in spite of what they said, the intention of each of America's leaders was to be defiant. Yet later in the book, when discussing John Edwards and Tom Daschle in the context of the eighth and ninth harbingers, he tries to make his case with exactly the opposite argument. There Cahn tries to make the case that in spite of what they said *and* in spite of what they intended, they were being defiant.

In this case, Cahn argues that context and intention are *everything*, but in that case, he assures the reader that context and intention mean *nothing*. He attempts to make the same point in both places but with contradictory logic. He cannot have it both ways.

Faulty logic

Cahn's theory concerning the "tower harbinger" is also burdened with another problem—a straw man argument.

The author tries to make it sound as if America's leaders should have been repentant as representatives before God on behalf of the entire nation. But these men were not the spiritual leaders of the nation, so they were not in a position to repent to God on behalf of *anyone*. Yet he bases his argument on the fact that they were not repentant. This is a classic straw man argument—misrepresent something and then attack the misrepresentation.

Neither did they know, nor could they have known, that God was expecting their repentance. They did not know, nor could they have known, that God was judging America just as He had Israel. Part of Cahn's argument is that he has just revealed this previously unknown truth for the first time in *The Harbinger*. Even if an argument could be made that they *should* have known (which is questionable), they did not. Therefore, they cannot be rightfully taken to task on this count. This is a straw man and cannot be legitimately used.

This leads to a second mistake in the author's logic. He falls prey to circular reasoning. Perhaps the 9/11 attacks were a judgment from God—perhaps they were not. Either way, part of Cahn's purpose for writing *The Harbinger* is to prove that the attacks *were* judgment. But by pointing out that these men should have been repentant, the author assumes what he is trying to prove—namely that America was under judgment. That is the very definition of circular reasoning.

Faulty exegesis and misleading exposition

Cahn's appeal to the Septuagint (the Koine Greek version of the Old Testament) as support for the fourth harbinger, "the tower," also needs to be examined.

[THE PROPHET] "The rebuilding of Ground Zero was supposed to have resulted in the tallest building in the world."

[KAPLAN] "A question," I said. "I understand the Tower as a symbol of the reconstruction, but is there any place in Isaiah that actually speaks of a tower?"

[THE PROPHET] "Centuries before the writing of the New Testament, the Hebrew Scriptures were translated into Greek. The result was a Greek version of the Hebrew Scriptures called the Septuagint. The Septuagint version of Isaiah 9:10 renders the rebuilding project in even more specific terms. It says this:

"'The bricks are fallen down . . . but come . . . *let us build for ourselves a TOWER.*'"[24]

Cahn rather nonchalantly uses a bit of linguistic sleight-of-hand to add support to his argument. It's true that the Septuagint is a translation of a Hebrew text, but it is not known which one.[25] What is known is that it was apparently not the Hebrew text that was used by the Jews of Jesus' day or as the basis for the Hebrew Old Testament of today, the Masoretic Text. (The abbreviation for the Septuagint is LXX and the abbreviation for the Masoretic Text is MT.)

The text of Isaiah 9:10 is one of many places where the text of the LXX and that of the MT do not exactly match up. The phrase "let us build for ourselves a tower" is only in the Greek LXX but not in the Hebrew MT. It's impossible to say whether or not it was in the Hebrew text used by the translators of the LXX. It is also impossible to say that these were the words of Isaiah himself. Therefore, it almost certainly should not be used as a technical linguistic argument to prove a point such as this one.

And the sleight-of-hand does not stop there. Cahn also fails to inform his readers that the rest of Isaiah 9:10 in the LXX is also different from the MT. He only quotes the part of the verse from the LXX that supports his argument, while ignoring the rest of it. The reader is therefore not aware that the LXX says that it is *Israel* who cuts down the sycamores, and that rather than planting cedars, *Israel* cuts those down as well! Cahn simply omits that phrase from the quote. The following is the entire verse in the LXX:

[SEPTUAGINT, ISAIAH 9:10] Bricks have fallen, but come, *let us hew stones and fell sycamores and cedars,* and let us build ourselves a tower.

It is obvious why it would have been difficult for Cahn to quote the entire verse from the LXX—the Greek translation actually *eliminates* both the sixth and seventh supposed harbingers. But the author can't have it both ways. It is extremely misleading and highly questionable methodology to pick one phrase out of a translation in order to prove a point when the passage as a whole has a very different meaning. The Word of God should not be handled in this manner, and one's audience should not be misled with such a dubious tactic.

FIFTH HARBINGER: THE GAZIT STONE

FACT CONCERNING ISRAEL: Israel would use the quarried and dressed stones to rebuild, rather than clay bricks, which had been used to build the original structures.

CLAIM CONCERNING AMERICA: A quarried Adirondack stone would be the cornerstone of the new World Trade Center tower.

Again, this has the feeling of yet another stretch in the author's attempt to demonstrate a parallel that simply doesn't exist. In Isaiah's prophecy, it is clear that in place of clay bricks being the primary building material, hewn stone would be used. However, the new Freedom Tower was never to be built with stone any more than the original structures were built with bricks.

It is true that a cornerstone (the "Freedom Stone") was quarried from the granite of the Adirondack mountains and set in place at Ground Zero on July 4, 2004. The original plan was that it would be four or five stories below street level as part of the foundation of the new World Trade Center building.[26]

However, after the plans for the building changed, it was given back and ended up sitting behind the Innovative Stone headquarters for years. On July 4, 2009, the Freedom Stone was rededicated and relocated to a memorial garden at the company's headquarters, which is located in Hauppauge, New York—almost 50 miles from Ground Zero.[27] Thus, it is not functioning to replace the bricks as in the prophecy and is not even part of the structure in any way.

This fact alone should be enough to show that this was not a fulfillment of Isaiah 9:10 or even a loose parallel to it. Yet in the book, although Cahn does note that the stone was removed from the WTC site, even this removal is stretched to suggest that this too is part of the fulfillment:

> [KAPLAN] "And what happened after," I asked, "after the stone was laid?"
>
> [THE PROPHET] "What happened after was especially striking. The rebuilding of Ground Zero had already become tangled in a continual stream of controversy, confusion, obstacles, dissension, and conflict. Even after the stone was set in place, the tower's construction would be challenged, halted, redrawn, renamed, and reversed. The plans to rebuild Ground Zero would be frustrated for years. Eventually they would remove the stone from Ground Zero altogether."
>
> [KAPLAN] "Strange," I said. "They removed the cornerstone, and after all those words."
>
> [THE PROPHET] "Strange and not so strange. *The plans of ancient Israel to defiantly rebuild itself would likewise be frustrated.* It would ultimately lead the nation to the point of destruction. The laying down of the Gazit Stone was one more link in a chain of judgment."[28]

So the claim is that not only was the laying of the stone part of the judgment, but its removal was also part of the judgment. It ultimately seems to make no difference what actually happens—everything is interpreted so that it supports and reinforces the author's foregone conclusions.

Another problem is the idea of the Freedom Stone being a "Gazit Stone." Except for its first mention, "Gazit Stone" is always capitalized in the book. Because of the fact that it is capitalized and the way it is spoken of throughout the dialogue between Kaplan and The Prophet, the average reader would easily assume that a "Gazit Stone" was a specially named ceremonial stone that was laid when Israel embarked on a building project.

> [THE PROPHET] " . . . the vow declares, 'The bricks have fallen, but we will rebuild with quarried stone.' So the rebuilding must

begin on the same site of the destruction. So the Gazit Stone must be brought to where the bricks had fallen, to the ground of the calamity. Thus, the quarried stone had to be brought back to Ground Zero. And so it was."

[KAPLAN] "And what happened at Ground Zero once they brought it back?"

[THE PROPHET] "There was a gathering there . . . various officials involved with the rebuilding, other leaders, and a gathering of guests and spectators. They were all focused on a single object—the Gazit Stone. The Gazit Stone most often took the form of a massive rectangular block of cut rock, so too the stone that was laid on the pavement of Ground Zero."

[KAPLAN] "A massive rectangular block of quarried stone . . . laid at Ground Zero?"

[THE PROPHET] "A twenty-ton massive rectangular block of quarried stone. The stone was to mark the beginning of the rebuilding."

[KAPLAN] "But we will rebuild with quarried stone."

[THE PROPHET] "Exactly. The stone of Isaiah's prophecy was another symbol of national defiance. So too they made the Gazit Stone of Ground Zero into a symbol."

This exchange is extremely misleading. The dialogue repeatedly gives the impression that the cornerstone, "The Freedom Stone," was some sort of specially designated stone that became the "Gazit Stone" as a parallel to Isaiah 9:10. In fact, there is simply no such thing as "a Gazit Stone" in any technical sense. *Gazit* is simply the generic Hebrew word for quarried or cut stone.[29]

In other words, the correct usage would be: "They built with gazit." It is both incorrect and misleading to say, as The Prophet does, "So too they made *the Gazit Stone* of Ground Zero into a symbol."

Although the laying of a cornerstone has both practical and symbolic significance, ancient Israel did not lay *a* "Gazit Stone." They built (or rebuilt) with *gazit*—it was simply the building material. Once again, Cahn uses a linguistic argument that does not hold up to scrutiny as is true of so many of the other arguments.

This is the way the Hebrew word is used in each of the eleven times it occurs in the Old Testament.[30] Nowhere does it speak of "a Gazit Stone," and "gazit" is never translated as "cornerstone." Except for one or two places, it refers to *all the stones in the structure.* In each of the six places where the cornerstone of a building is in view (either literally or figuratively)[31] the only word that is used is *pinnah* ("corner"), except for one place (Job 38:6), where it is used together with *eben* ("stone") to also mean "cornerstone."

Gazit has no ceremonial or symbolic significance in Isaiah 9:10 or in any other Old Testament passage. The supposed parallel is a manufactured one. It is simply not a harbinger.

SIXTH HARBINGER: THE SYCAMORE

FACT CONCERNING ISRAEL: Many or most of the fig-mulberry trees (sycamores) were cut down by the Assyrians as part of their assaults on Israel.

CLAIM CONCERNING AMERICA: A lone American sycamore stood in the courtyard of St. Paul's Chapel in the shadow of the World Trade Center and was knocked down as a result of the collapse of the buildings and flying debris.

This is yet another forced parallel that does not withstand closer examination. First, the sycamore (fig-mulberry) of ancient Israel and the American sycamore are two completely different trees that are unrelated in any way.[32] They are not the same species (*Ficus sycomorus* versus *Platanus occidentalis*). They are not in the same genus (*Ficus* versus *Platanus*) nor even in the same family (*Moraceae* versus *Platanaceae*). In spite of this, the author tries to make the connection on a linguistic basis. He argues that the trees in ancient Israel were sycamores to them, while a different tree in America is a sycamore to us.

> [THE PROPHET] "In each case, the ancient and the modern, the leaders speak in the tongue of their people and nation. The Harbinger is translated into the context of the nation in which it appears and to the people to whom it is directed. *So too with the sign of the Sycamore. It was a translation.*"

[KAPLAN] "A translation . . . how?"

[THE PROPHET] "The tree matches the nation . . . the land. The tree of Isaiah 9:10 was endemic to Israel. So the tree of 9/11 was endemic to America."

[KAPLAN] "But you said it was a sycamore."

[THE PROPHET] "It's classified under the genus *platanus*. But it's known by its common English name . . . sycamore. It was a sycamore."

[KAPLAN] "But . . . "

[THE PROPHET] "Yes, you were right, Nouriel. The Middle Eastern sycamore doesn't naturally grow in the American Northeast. But there exists a version of the sycamore that does—the English sycamore."

[KAPLAN] "The English sycamore . . . a translation of the Harbinger."

[THE PROPHET] "And it was the English sycamore that happened to be growing on the little plot of land at the border of Ground Zero."

Again, this exchange is misleading. The tree in Israel is a *fruit-bearing* tree, with the English translation ultimately coming from the Greek for "fig-mulberry" which is *sycomoros*. However, this tree is *shaqam* in Hebrew. So it is not legitimate to claim that this tree was a "sycamore" to the ancient Israelites, who lived long before the influence of the Greek Empire. It was a fig-mulberry—it was a *shaqam* to them.

In contrast, the American sycamore, as stated before, is not botanically related in any way to the fig-mulberry. There is no semantic connection. Of course, both trees carry the same name—but this is true only for *English-speakers*—not for Hebrew-speakers.

The following example from English and Hungarian illustrates the fundamental flaw in the author's linguistic argument. In Hungarian, the word *kocsi* (kó-chi) can mean either *automobile* or *wagon* (horse-drawn), but they cannot be used interchangeably in English. Even if someone were to install an engine to power a horse-drawn wagon in order to make it *auto-mobile*, it would still not be an *automobile*.

Yet this is precisely the type of mistake that Cahn makes in *The Harbinger*. It's true that automobiles and "auto-mobile" war wagons are both vehicles, just as sycamores and fig-mulberries are both trees. However, automobiles and wagons are more closely "related" to one another than are these two types of trees.

Furthermore, in the case of Israel, the fig-mulberry trees were *cut down* intentionally by the Assyrians, possibly for their wood to be used in siege engines, or perhaps to complete the scene of utter destruction. Either way, many, or perhaps all of the fig-mulberry trees were destroyed by the invaders, being specific targets, apparently as part of their military strategy. Their destruction was a significant blow to Israel as a nation.

However, in the case of the 9/11 attacks, there was just a single American sycamore at St. Paul's Chapel, which was not a target, was not cut down, and was not intentionally destroyed. It was collateral damage and had absolutely no impact on the nation—except for perhaps the fact that its destruction was a *blessing*. How was it a blessing? It seems that the tree actually shielded St. Paul's Chapel by absorbing the force of the blast, protecting it from any significant loss, although all the surrounding buildings were either destroyed or sustained tremendous damage.[33]

Again, there is none but the most superficial connection with the trees in Isaiah 9:10. The sycamore cannot reasonably be considered to be a harbinger.

SEVENTH HARBINGER: THE EREZ TREE

FACT CONCERNING ISRAEL: Israel declared they would plant cedars of Lebanon to replace sycamores in defiance of the Assyrians who cut them down and in defiance of God who had sent them to judge the nation.

CLAIM CONCERNING AMERICA: A Norway spruce was planted at Ground Zero to replace the sycamore as an act of defiance just as did ancient Israel.

Cahn once again goes to great lengths to connect current events to Isaiah's prophecy. He uses a scientific argument that appears to be straightforward on the surface. However, the complexity has been obscured by a few well-placed "broad brush strokes."

With the sycamores of the sixth harbinger, Cahn uses a linguistic argument that does not account for the science involved. His argument overlooks the fact that the American sycamore and the fig-mulberry are not even in the same botanical family.

However, with the Erez tree, his scientific argument does not fit the way *erez* is used in the Bible. His argument depends on the fact that the spruce at Ground Zero and the *erez(im)* in ancient Israel *are* in the same botanical family. He can't have it both ways.

As previously, Cahn tries to make it sound as if he has an open-and-shut case, which he does not. He mishandles the scientific evidence, but even more important, his argument goes beyond a lack of biblical evidence. It *contradicts* the biblical evidence. In addition, he again fails to accurately convey the historical context of the events.

First, Cahn tries to persuade the reader that the spruce that replaced the sycamore at Ground Zero exactly matched the cedars in Isaiah 9:10 when The Prophet says, "It is a *particular kind* of cone-bearing evergreen."[34] But he then immediately reverses direction by arguing that the match is due to the fact that cedar and spruce trees are both part of the same broad category. He cites a commentary for support: "The Hebrew *erez* rendered 'cedar' in all English versions, is most likely a generic word for the *pine family*."[35] Then comes the following exchange:

[THE PROPHET] "The Erez Tree would fall under the botanical classification of *pinacea*."

[KAPLAN] "*Pinacea*. And what," I asked, "does pinacea refer to specifically?"

[THE PROPHET] "The cedar, the spruce, the pine, and the fir."

[KAPLAN] "So the most accurate identification of the Hebrew word *erez* would be *pinacea tree*."

[THE PROPHET] "Yes. The most botanically precise translation of the vow would be, 'But we will plant *pinacea trees* in their place.'"[36]

So, which is it? Does the spruce match the *erez* tree because it is a particular *kind* of tree? Or does it match because *erez* refers only to a broad *category*? The remainder of Cahn's argument hinges on *erez* referring only to the broad category of *Pinacea* family, or *pine tree*. But that is not the way *erez* is used in the Bible.

The biblical evidence

A careful biblical study of *erez* reveals that the spruce at Ground Zero is not parallel to the cedars of ancient Israel. The results of this study are summarized here:

1. In Isaiah 9:10, "cedars" is the translation of the plural of the Hebrew word *erez* (*erezim*).

2. *Erez* is used in sixty-nine verses of the Old Testament and is *always* translated "cedar" in twenty different English translations and revisions.[37] Hundreds of theologians and Hebrew scholars all reached the consensus that *erez* is always "cedar." *(Note: This is not an endorsement of all the translations consulted for this specific purpose.)*

This raises the next question: "*What type* of cedar trees did the biblical writers mean when they used *erez*?" Were they just cedars in general or a specific type of cedar?

1. Twenty-three of the sixty-nine verses identify *erez* as the *cedar of Lebanon* because the word *Lebanon* is either in the verse or the nearby context.[38]

2. Twenty-seven of the remaining forty-six verses connect *erez* to construction and buildings, mostly the temple and royal palaces, where only cedars of Lebanon were used.[39] Three of the uses are figurative but are still part of a building metaphor.[40]

3. Seven of the remaining nineteen verses connect *erez* with religious activity: five with purification,[41] one with a sacrifice,[42] and one with making an idol.[43] (Some have suggested that the *juniper* may be in view in Leviticus,[44] but it is never translated that way.)

4. In six of the remaining twelve verses, *erez* is used figuratively. But in each case, the cedar of Lebanon must be in view. It depicts the glory of Israel's camp in the wilderness,[45] describes the tail of *behemoth* in Job,[46] and refers to the majestic cedars.[47] Only Psalm 148:9 *might* refer to cedars in general, but the only cedar found in the region of ancient Israel is the cedar of Lebanon.[48]

5. In the last six verses, the trees are *planted erez* trees. This includes Isaiah 9:10, where it seems clear that specifically cedars of Lebanon will be planted—not pine trees in general.

6. The Bible does refer to other conifers but never as *erez*. Other words are translated as *fir*,[49] *cypress*,[50] and *pine*,[51] but never as *cedar*.

7. *Erez* occurs in some verses with other *Pinacea* trees, but each refers to a different type of tree, showing that *erez* cannot be a generic word for a broad category. For example:

Isaiah 41:19—

I will plant in the wilderness the cedar and the acacia tree, the myrtle and the oil tree; I will set in the desert the cypress and the pine and the box tree together . . .

    cedar = *erez*[52] (a *Pinacea*)
    cypress = *berosh* (perhaps better: *fir - a Pinacea*)
    pine = *tidhar* (perhaps *Aleppo pine - a Pinacea*)[53]
    box tree = *teashshur* (*evergreen*, but perhaps not a *Pinacea*)

Even though not all trees of the Bible can be identified with certainty, it is clear that the author had specific trees in mind—not just broad families.

The biblical evidence overwhelmingly shows that the *erez tree* is exclusively the *cedar of Lebanon*. There is no amazing biblical coincidence between the cedar of Isaiah 9:10 and the Norway spruce at Ground Zero (as the author would have the reader believe). There is no match. There is no parallel. And there is no harbinger.

The scientific evidence

Cahn's reasoning reveals that he is depending on the *taxonomic* classification system to make his case. The taxonomic system is based on a hierarchy of seven ranks for classifying all living things on earth, which are:

kingdom > phyla > class > order > family > genus > species [54]

The first problem with appealing to this classification system is that it is based *exclusively* on evolutionary theory. In addition, as evolutionary theory evolves, so does the classification system itself, and it can change significantly over time. A lack of consensus often exists about relationships within and between ranks. Therefore, disagreements about groupings arise from differences of opinion with the result that the system can be very subjective.[55]

The following statement perfectly illustrates one of the major biblical problems with this evolutionary-based system:

> The taxonomic tree above tells us that humans and armadillos are related, but not closely. We share the same class, but belong to different orders.[56]

This directly contradicts the biblical view of the way God has grouped life on earth—which is "according to kind." Humans are simply not related to armadillos in *any* way.

1 Corinthians 15:39—

All flesh is not the same flesh, but there is one kind of flesh of men, another flesh of animals, another of fish, and another of birds.

The Creation account reveals important additional information about the grouping of plants by kind:

Genesis 1:11—

Then God said, "Let the earth bring forth grass, the herb that yields seed, and the fruit tree that yields fruit according to its kind, whose seed is in itself, on the earth"; and it was so.

As indicated by the reference to *fruit* and *seed* as the criteria for grouping by *kind*, the biblical biological classification system has boundaries marked off by reproductive compatibility. Among animals, even within kinds, there are often reproductive dead-ends because of sterile offspring (such as mules). If organisms (in this case plants) are not compatible in the realm of reproduction, they constitute a different *kind*.

The Norway spruce planted at Ground Zero is biblically a *different kind* of tree than the cedars of Lebanon in Isaiah 9:10. Although the Bible is not a scientific textbook, it is accurate in those matters of science about which it speaks. Consequently, based on the authority of the Word of God, there is no amazing coincidence. There is no match. There is no parallel. And there is no harbinger.

Even if one were to accept the taxonomical classification system rather than the "kind system" of the Bible, the situation would be no better. As noted previously, the cedar of Lebanon is classified in the *Pinacea* family. However, it is more narrowly classified in the genus *Cedrus* and of the species *Cedrus libani*.[57] In contrast, the tree that was planted at Ground Zero was also in the *Pinacea* family, but it was of the genus *Picea* and the species *Picea abies*.[58]

It should also be noted that even though *Pinacea* is technically in the "pine family," this is using "family" in the taxonomic sense, which is not the way we often think of things being in the same family. Pine trees themselves are a separate genus (*Pinus*) which is only a subset of *Pinacea*. Only evolutionary theory suggests that the *Pinus* and *Cedrus* genera are somehow related with a common ancestor at the family level of *Pinacea*.

Since *The Harbinger* purports to convey *biblical* truth, it seems very misguided to rely on an unbiblical theory of origins and development of life on earth to establish fulfilled prophecy. This is not to suggest that Cahn supports or believes in evolution. And it's unlikely that he realizes the full implications of his argument. Nonetheless, he should be held accountable for each of the arguments he uses to support his theories. (It's unfortunate that a work of fiction needs to be so carefully examined biblically and scientifically, but the way that Cahn attempts to support his theories makes it necessary.)

Biblically, the ultimate question concerns both Isaiah's and the Lord's intent in Isaiah's prophecy. The text makes it clear that Isaiah was referring to replacing one specific kind of tree (fig-mulberry trees) with another specific kind of tree (cedars of Lebanon). He was not prophesying that just any tree that might be called a "sycamore" in another language would be replaced by just any tree within the taxonomic rank of the *Pinacea* family, such as a Norway spruce.

Neither was Isaiah's prophecy a warning to be fulfilled with a couple of relatively insignificant symbolic events such as the exchange of one unimportant tree for another. The Assyrian army totally decimated the countryside, wiping out untold numbers of fig-mulberry trees across the land. In turn, Israel would replace them with the much stronger and more majestic cedars of Lebanon, symbolizing Israel's defiance and determination to return to her glory days.

It's puzzling how this could be identified as a precise match and literal fulfillment when there is no amazing *scientific* coincidence. Again, there is no match. There is no parallel. And there is no harbinger.

The historical evidence

The third major problem with Cahn's theory of *The Erez Tree* harbinger concerns Israel's attitude and unmitigated act of defiance. Israel wanted to show the Assyrians that their attacks had neither permanently destroyed the nation nor their resolve to survive all attempts to annihilate them. Yet Israel also knew that the Assyrians were merely instruments in the hands of God, who was severely judging them. Their intentional defiance was ultimately directed at the Lord.

Likewise, Cahn portrays the placement of the Tree of Hope (the Norway spruce) at Ground Zero as an equally significant act of defiance toward God. This is despite the complete lack of supporting evidence. Those at the ceremony simply *were not defying God.* They were not necessarily even showing defiance toward America's enemies at that point in time. They were focused on bringing a message of comfort and hope to the soul of a nation that had not fully recovered from 9/11. However, as before, the author disregards this in favor of trying to create more support for his theories:

> [THE PROPHET] "The Erez Tree becomes another symbol of the nation and its defiance—a living symbol of their confidence in their national resurgence, their tree of hope."

> [KAPLAN] "A tree of hope, but not a good hope."

[THE PROPHET] "No," he replied, "a prideful, self-centered, and godless hope. What they saw as a tree of hope was, in reality, a harbinger of judgment."[59]

* * *

[KAPLAN] "They replaced the fallen Sycamore with the Erez Tree!"

[THE PROPHET] "The sign of a nation's false hope and defiance before God."

[KAPLAN] "It's like something out of a movie . . . it's surreal!"

[THE PROPHET] "Except that it's real."

[KAPLAN] "Who was behind the decision to do that?" I asked.

[THE PROPHET] "No one," he answered. "No one in the sense of any one person making it all happen or trying to fulfill the prophecy."

[KAPLAN] "No one had any idea what they were doing?"

[THE PROPHET] "No one."[60]

Cahn imposes a clearly wrong interpretation on the events surrounding the placing of the Tree of Hope and misrepresents those who were involved. However, even two years after 9/11, the spirit at the dedication ceremony at St. Paul's Chapel was consistent with what had happened at the church during the year following the terrorist attacks. In September 2002, *National Geographic* published an article by a minister at the church in which he described his experience during that year:

> More than 5,000 people used their special gifts to transform St. Paul's into a place of rest and refuge. Musicians, clergy, podiatrists, lawyers, soccer moms, and folks of every imaginable type poured coffee, swept floors, took out the trash, and served more than half a million meals. Emerging at St. Paul's was a dynamic I think of as a reciprocity of gratitude, a circle of thanksgiving—in which volunteers and rescue and recovery workers tried to outdo each other with acts of kindness and love, leaving both giver and receiver changed. This circle of gratitude was infectious, and I hope it continues to spread. In fact, I hope it turns into an epidemic.[61]

That minister's heart is clearly reflected in the words he spoke just a few days after the attacks: "But we would gladly give up St. Paul's to have saved just one life across the street."[62] Even someone who might have sharp theological disagreements with whatever might be preached on any given Sunday at that church can readily see there was no spirit of defiance against God in this place—intentional or otherwise. It is simply unreasonable and misleading to suggest that the placement, dedication, and lighting ceremonies for the Tree of Hope were any different.

The 21-foot Norway spruce was lowered into the ground on November 22, 2003. This was followed by a prayer service and lighting ceremony on November 29, when St. Paul's was filled to capacity.[63] Rather than an unintentional act of defiance toward God, it was an intentional act of worship and reliance on Him. Although some might argue that many there were not actually worshiping the God of the Bible, when it comes to assessing motives the important point is that they believed that they were. It is not their theology that is in question.

Many internet articles purport to quote part of the prayer of dedication as including a reference to "the divine in all of us." Of course, if true, this statement would be heresy. However, as of this writing, despite extensive research by this author, the original source of that prayer has not been located. It appears that most if not all writers may be referencing a message by Jonathan Cahn at his church, but this has not been confirmed. Unfortunately, the endnote referenced on page 94 of *The Harbinger*, which is also said to be a quote from the dedication ceremony, only mentions the name of the speaker and cites no source for the quote.

However, even if true, it would be difficult to characterize this as *defiance with a malicious heart*. Although Israel's defiance would have fallen into the category of an intentional "high-handed sin," such was not the case at the dedication of the Tree of Hope.

The plaque at the site of the Tree of Hope has the following inscription:

> Ground Zero workers helped plant this Norway spruce on November 22, 2003, in place of a giant sycamore that was struck down during the collapse of the World Trade Center. In a special Thanksgiving service, St. Paul's dedicated the new tree as "The Tree of Hope," *a reminder and affirmation of the power of love in the face of tragedy*.[64]

There is nothing about any aspect of this theorized harbinger that constitutes an amazing *historical* coincidence. There is no match. There is no parallel. And there is no harbinger.

Isaiah 9:10 fulfilled in America?

And finally, concerning the Erez tree, it must be noted once again that Cahn has at times tried to distance himself from his own words in the book by stating that Isaiah 9:10 is not a prophecy about America. However, it is virtually impossible to reconcile this claim with the following exchange:

> [THE PROPHET] "The new tree was set into position to stand on the same spot where once had stood the Sycamore of Ground Zero."
>
> [KAPLAN] "What was it? What kind of tree?"
>
> [THE PROPHET] "The most natural thing to have done would have been to replace the one Sycamore with another. *But the prophecy required* that the fallen Sycamore be replaced with a tree of an entirely different nature."[65]

The prophecy in Isaiah 9:10 cannot require anything to happen *in America* if it was not given *to America*. Yet repeatedly Cahn insists that each of the harbinger events *had to happen* in America after 9/11 because the Isaiah passage *required them to happen*. Once again, there is no amazing prophetic coincidence. There is no match. There is no parallel. And there is no harbinger

EIGHTH HARBINGER: THE UTTERANCE

FACT CONCERNING ISRAEL: Words of defiant pride and arrogance were uttered by Israel after the Assyrian invasion as prophesied in Isaiah 9:9-10.

CLAIM CONCERNING AMERICA: When America's leaders in Washington, D.C., repeat the words of Isaiah 9:10, they are proclaiming a vow that officially pronounces God's judgment against the United States.

Once again, the author belies the fact that he truly does believe there is a direct connection between ancient Israel and present-day America:

> [THE PROPHET] "Well done, Nouriel. So what would we expect to find in Washington DC?"

> [KAPLAN] "Some link between this city and the ancient vow," I said. "*Somehow Isaiah 9:10 has to be connected to Washington DC.*"[66]

This does not appear to be simply part of the fictional storyline, but rather a connection that Cahn affirms time and again throughout the book. The evidence continues to mount that he believes that in some way Isaiah 9:10 was not only to Israel but was also to, about, and for the United States. Cahn uses the idea that "Somehow Isaiah 9:10 has to be connected to Washington DC" to set up his theory concerning the eighth harbinger.

John Edwards's "prophetic utterance"

On September 11, 2004, then vice-presidential candidate John Edwards was speaking at the Congressional Black Caucus Prayer Breakfast. As was said of those involved with the placement of the Tree of Hope at Ground Zero, Cahn frames Edwards's words as part of an unwitting act of defiance. However, an honest reading of the entire speech[67] makes it clear that not only was defiance of God the furthest thing from his mind, but neither was he unwittingly using defiant words (as can be seen in the following excerpts from the speech). So if defiance was not in his words and if it was not in his heart and mind, then where was it? Unfortunately, this is just one more thing that has been made up.

> Good morning. Today, on this day of remembrance and mourning, *we have the Lord's word to get us through.* "The bricks have fallen, but we will build with dressed stones; the sycamores have been cut down, but we will put cedars in their place."
>
> * * *
>
> Today, a town gathers in front of their church. It is a town where so many—53—were taken before their time. For a week after that September day, the Lord's doors were open. *The Lord's doors were open for that hour of loneliness* just before dawn . . .
>
> * * *

They will lay a wreath. They will pray, "Onward, soldier, you answered your calling here, but *your work is not done in the Lord's house.*" And *they will pray* for those whose wounds have not healed—the burns that cause them great pain every time they reach out to hold their wife's hand until the stars rise and the night falls on this day in September...

* * *

At this hour and all day long, strangers will follow the Lord's wish. In memory and in the hope that goodwill and grace will always triumph out of tragedy, they will give...

* * *

At this breakfast, *our prayers will be heard and answered* for those who still need comfort...

* * *

Thank you and *God bless you, the families and friends who mourn, and our great United States of America.*[68]

Not a single hint of defiance can be read into Edwards's words. Defiance most certainly was not on the hearts and minds of those in attendance at the prayer breakfast that morning either. Yet in spite of all evidence to the contrary, the following dialogue explains what Cahn believes really happened that day:

> [KAPLAN] "It wasn't about the motive or the intention of the one doing it, but the fact that it was done . . . that it happened. It happened because *it had to happen.* It was another replaying of the ancient mystery. What the speaker intended to say was irrelevant. The words came out because those were *the words that had to be spoken.* The vow had to be proclaimed, the words of the ancient leaders over the ancient calamity *had to be proclaimed* by an American leader over 9/11. *And by doing so, the two nations, the ancient and the modern, were bound together. The utterance would join the Assyrian invasion to 9/11 and America's post-9/11 defiance to Israel's defiance in the face of God's judgment.*"

Jonathan Cahn contends that Edwards was openly defying God but did not realize he was doing so. Cahn does the same thing concerning Tom Daschle in the next chapter. Based on nothing more than a need to fit his harbinger theory, the author contends that although Edwards and Daschle both intended to say one thing, their words carried a far different meaning—a meaning that they did not intend and a meaning that no one who heard either speech would have understood or even remotely considered.

John Edwards is obviously no Bible scholar, and his speech writers clearly mishandled Isaiah 9:10 when using it as a springboard for the speech. Unfortunately, this was arguably no worse than the way Jonathan Cahn has handled this passage throughout the book and in every interview as he directly connects Isaiah's prophecy to the United States of America. Thus he contends that Edwards was precisely the chosen vessel whom the Lord inspired on precisely that morning in precisely that speech to precisely fulfill Isaiah's prophecy. In other words, in spite of Edwards's clear intentions, God *caused* John Edwards to unknowingly pronounce judgment on America.

Yet inexplicably, within the space of a couple of sentences, Cahn again tries to have it both ways. On one hand, he tries to argue that it couldn't have been a coincidence because Isaiah 9:10 is so obscure. On the other hand, he argues that Edwards's speech writers used the passage because they found so many examples of others who had used it on similar occasions.

> [KAPLAN] "So," I replied, "out of over thirty thousand verses . . . that's the one he chose? And you said it was obscure . . . that even people who read the Bible every day would probably have no idea it existed."
>
> [THE PROPHET] "That is correct," he replied.
>
> [KAPLAN] "So how on earth did he end up choosing that particular verse?"
>
> [THE PROPHET] "How was the Sycamore cut down?" he asked. "Through a series of twists and quirks. But now the twists and quirks take place in the realm of speech writing, in the searching through quotations deemed most appropriate for such occasions, in the borrowing of passages and quotes from other proclamations and speeches. . . ."[69]

This manner of contradictory logic plagues *The Harbinger* throughout the text.

John Edwards's lack of conscious defiance would clearly undermine

Cahn's theory, were it not for yet another theoretical element that he injected into the discussion in connection with Daschle's speech in the next chapter concerning the ninth harbinger—that the words of the Senate majority leader were actually *inspired by God*. There Cahn contends that not only was *the Lord* inspiring Daschle to speak out in defiance against Him but also that He was causing Daschle to *prophesy judgment* against America. However, this element is not found in Isaiah 9:10 concerning Israel's leaders, and it is impossible to defend in the context of the speeches of these two men. This part of Cahn's theory will be examined in the next chapter.

The utterance as a biblical vow

Cahn brings yet another concept into his argument that lacks both biblical and historical support when he refers to Isaiah 9:10 and Edwards's words as a *vow*. The idea that both include *vows* is a crucial part of Cahn's theory—so much so that he uses the word 100 times in the book.[70]

As with his other ideas, concepts, and theories, Cahn presents this one in such a way that most readers will probably never give a second thought as to whether or not the author has used the term *vow* biblically. He has not. And because of this, he has wrongly concluded that Isaiah 9:10 and John Edwards's speech both contain a vow. They do not.

Cahn's less-than-careful use of biblical terminology shows up in multiple places throughout *The Harbinger*. The previously noted misuse of the concept of God's *hedge of protection* is a prime example. These are not trivial, inconsequential matters. In order to make a biblical case, especially for something with implications as far-reaching as this book, the burden for being biblically accurate falls squarely on the author's shoulders.

With a couple of exceptions, the Hebrew words translated as *vow* in the Old Testament are *neder* (noun form) and *nadar* (verb form). *Vow* (*neder*) is a well-understood and very specific Hebrew concept as demonstrated by its consistent usage by the biblical writers—which is never as broadly defined as Cahn uses the term.

In English, *vow* can be used as a synonym for any type of oath or promise. An oath, promise, or vow in general is simply a declaration of the intent to do something. For example, it can be used in the noun form: "He took an oath/made a vow to uphold the law." Or in the verb form: "She promised/vowed that she would return."

This is also the way *vow* is used in the Bible—with one very important additional aspect: A vow *always* involves God in some way (and, of course, it is always intentional). This generally happens in one of two ways. A biblical vow is sometimes a declaration directly to God in which the person declares his intention to do something for Him, because of Him, in faithfulness to Him, and so on. A biblical vow can also be a declaration of intent to another person, with God invoked as a witness to the oath or promise. A biblical vow always involves God directly and intentionally.

Israel's declaration in Isaiah 9:10 does not call upon God as a witness nor does it seem to be directed to God. In context, it seems to be directed to the people of Israel in the same way that a politician would make a promise that he is going to do something or make certain that something will happen. In fact, it seems that a major problem was that they had *excluded* God from their thinking. It was a promise to be sure, but it was not a biblical vow.

It might be argued that John Edwards came closer to making a vow than did Israel's leaders because at least his words were in the general context of acknowledging God and His Word (i.e., Isaiah 9:10) at a prayer breakfast. However, his speech was not directed to God, nor did he invoke God as a witness to an oath to rebuild.

What is more, Edwards did not even actually make any promises in his speech. He made no declaration that America would rebuild what had been physically destroyed. Throughout his speech, Edwards used Isaiah only metaphorically, and even at that, it was not a very good metaphor for his main theme, which was about how people were coping with their losses three years after 9/11. Anyone who takes time to read his speech can quickly see that it had nothing to do with rebuilding at all. He made no promises or declarations that day. He made no biblical vow, and there was no "prophetic utterance."

Just as before, Cahn reads his theories and conclusions into multiple events in order to connect dots that are not there and then presents them as undeniable facts. Consequently, just as is true of the previous harbingers, the eighth harbinger is only one of the author's own making. It does not exist. There can be little doubt that the supposed utterance by John Edwards is not a harbinger.

NINTH HARBINGER: THE PROPHECY

FACT CONCERNING ISRAEL: Isaiah 9:10 as a whole was a prophecy, a word from God through the prophet Isaiah, concerning what was to befall Israel.

CLAIM CONCERNING AMERICA: By quoting Isaiah's prophecy against Israel, America's leaders were likewise prophesying judgment against the United States in the wake of 9/11.

Cahn's explanation of the ninth harbinger, "The Prophecy," is even more misleading than what he said in the documentary about the speeches given by America's leaders (noted in an earlier chapter). Concerning Senate Majority Leader Tom Daschle's speech on 9/12/2001, the day following the attack, Cahn gives the impression that Daschle concluded his speech by quoting Isaiah 9:10:

> [THE PROPHET] ". . . At the end of the speech would come the climax. These are the words proclaimed by the Senate majority leader on Capitol Hill, the morning after 9/11, to present and sum up the nation's response to the calamity. Listen . . ."

> [THE PROPHET QUOTING DASCHLE] "I know that there is only the smallest measure of inspiration that can be taken from this devastation, but there is a passage in the Bible from Isaiah that I think speaks to all of us at times like this . . .

> *The bricks have fallen down,*
> *But we will rebuild with dressed stone;*
> *The fig trees have been felled,*
> *But we will replace them with cedars."*

This is where Cahn leaves it in *The Harbinger*. However, that is not how Daschle ended his speech.

In the documentary by *WND*, Cahn goes even further to explicitly identify what he says are the closing words of Daschle's speech when at the 44:38 mark on DVD #1 he says:

> [CAHN] And he *closes the speech with these words*; he said this . . .
> [cuts to a video clip of Daschle's speech]

[DASCHLE] "That is what we will do and we will rebuild. We will recover." [cuts back to Cahn]

[CAHN] "That is what we will do." He is referring to Isaiah 9:10—he just said it. So what is it . . . it is mind-boggling. What he's saying is America's policy, now, America's course will be Isaiah 9:10. And this is prophetic in so many ways . . ."[71]

However, Daschle did not end his speech with this statement either. He added two more sentences—which were not included in either the book or the documentary:

[DASCHLE] "The people of America will stand together because the people of America have always stood together, and those of us who are privileged to serve this great nation will stand with you. *God bless the people of America.*"[72]

By invoking God with the intent to comfort Americans and by using the Bible (albeit wrongly), Daschle's intention was clearly not defiance of God—it was exactly the opposite. The decision to edit out the last two sentences of the Senate majority leader's speech and the failure to at least mention them is very misleading, if not worse. But there is more:

[THE PROPHET] "The Ninth Harbinger," he said. "In the wake of the calamity, the nation issues its response in the form of a vow. The vow sets the nation on a course of defiance, a course that ends in judgment. *The words of the vow become part of a prophetic revelation* given to the nation as a whole, an indictment of its rebellion, a foretelling of its future, a warning of its judgment. The Ninth Harbinger: the Prophecy."

[KAPLAN] "Then according to the mystery there would have to have been *a prophetic word given* in the wake of 9/11 . . . to fall on the nation."[73]

Now Cahn is claiming that Daschle was fulfilling *a revelatory prophetic role* and publicly pronouncing judgment on the United States of America:

[KAPLAN] "But he was identifying America as a nation under judgment."

[THE PROPHET] "Yes, unwittingly."

[KAPLAN] "The majority leader of the United States Senate was publicly pronouncing judgment on America."

[THE PROPHET] "Blindly," he replied, "having no idea what he was pronouncing. As far as he knew, he was only delivering an inspiring speech."

[KAPLAN] "But unknowingly playing his part in a prophetic mystery."

[THE PROPHET] "Yes . . . and so the words of the ancient vow were now officially joined to America and 9/11. And just as Isaiah's recording of the vow transformed it into a matter of national record and a prophetic word for all the people, so now the same words were officially recorded in the Annals of Congress as a matter of national record."[74]

How could Daschle have been proclaiming a prophetic word from God to the people of the United States? Cahn has an unexpected (and problematic) explanation for that question.

[KAPLAN] "So someone can prophesy without being a prophet. How does that happen?"

[THE PROPHET] "The word is inspiration. When a prophet speaks, he does so *under the inspiration of the Spirit*. But prophets aren't the only ones who can speak or act under inspiration. The Bible itself is called the inspired Word of God because it was written by those under the inspiration of God's Spirit—not only by prophets."[75]

By this point in the book, Cahn has overwhelmed his readers with such a vast array of "inexplicable coincidences" that can only be attributed to the hand of God that apparently he is able to get away with just about anything—no matter how bizarre or unbiblical. He defends the indefensible theory that Daschle was prophesying by referring to an incident recorded in John chapter 11 concerning Caiaphas the high priest.

After Jesus had raised Lazarus from the dead, Caiaphas, by virtue of his office as high priest, unwittingly prophesied that Jesus would die for the nation of Israel in a sense beyond what he actually intended:

John 11:49–52—

> And one of them, Caiaphas, being high priest that year, said to them, "You know nothing at all, nor do you consider that it is expedient for us that one man should die for the people, and not that the whole nation should perish." Now this he did not say on his own authority; but being high priest that year he prophesied that Jesus would die for the nation, and not for that nation only, but also that He would gather together in one the children of God who were scattered abroad.

Question: *How does a reader of the Bible know that Caiaphas's words were inspired by God?*

Answer: *The Holy Spirit has revealed it in the inspired text of John's Gospel.*

If the Holy Spirit had not chosen to reveal what was going on through John's writings, it would have been impossible to know for certain that God was behind this. It might make for an interesting discussion, but no one could responsibly proclaim with any confidence that God had caused this to happen. Apart from revelation, it would be nothing more than speculation.

Question: *How does Cahn know that Daschle's words were inspired by God?*

Answer: *He does not, and he cannot, unless God has revealed it to him.*

If God did do this, then when and where and by what means did He do so? If true, this needs to be documented, and Cahn needs to discuss it publicly. Yet as shown earlier, the author has denied the claim that he is a prophet.

Unfortunately, Cahn has raised his speculation to the level of a prophetic declaration that "God did such and such. . . ." However, to declare with this level of certainty that God did something that He arguably did not do is not significantly different from declaring that God said something He did not say—which is the very definition of a false prophet.

Perhaps one might wonder if there are enough similarities to legitimately compare and correlate what America's leaders did with what Caiaphas did. But even a cursory examination reveals that this is not the case:

1. Israel was supposed to be a theocracy, with a king serving as God's regent on the earth over His covenant people. There is no equivalent situation in America, unless one presumes at the outset that America is also in a special covenant relationship with God and ordained to be a theocracy with theocratic leaders who would speak and act on their behalf.

2. In Israel, as is true of any theocracy, the political and religious realms were inseparably linked. In America, not only is there no such linkage, but by virtue of the Constitution, any such linkage is precluded.

3. God used Caiaphas to prophesy by virtue of his position as high priest that year—he was the highest spiritual leader of the entire nation. He represented everyone in Israel to God. America's leaders are not spiritual leaders in any sense and certainly do not represent Americans directly before God.

4. The incident with Caiaphas appears to be unique. There are no precedents nor repetition of what happened with him that are recorded anywhere in Scripture. This makes it impossible to establish this as a *pattern* of the way God works.

5. The true meaning of Caiaphas's words did not contradict either what he intended to say or what he actually said. They simply carried more significance than he or those around him realized. In stark contrast, Cahn maintains that Daschle's words carried exactly the *opposite* meaning of both what he intended and what he did say.

6. This claim actually introduces a significant issue that might not be readily apparent. Allegorical interpretation is a hermeneutical approach that disconnects the real meaning of a passage from what the words of the text actually say. The problem with this approach is that there is no objective way to know if one's interpretation is correct. This is precisely what Cahn has done with the words of John Edwards and Tom Daschle. The meaning that he assigns to their speeches is completely disconnected from what the words *actually say*.

An important principle that must always be kept in mind when studying the Bible is: *If a proposed theological or spiritual idea does not come from the biblical text, then someone made it up.* This is the problem with the allegorical approach because the meaning does not come from the text. However, as a literary principle, this is also applicable to anything that has been written or said. Therefore, it must be concluded that the meaning assigned to Edwards's and Daschle's speeches has been made up.

Once again, the author's exposition of the biblical text does not stand up to scrutiny, and the supposed parallel is simply not there. His conclusions constitute nothing more than speculation without the slightest textual or historical support. And if such a parallel does not exist, then neither does the Ninth Harbinger. Daschle's speech, "The Prophecy," is not a harbinger for America.

CHAPTER 11

THE SECOND SHAKING

THE HARBINGER has two major parts. The first part (chapters 1-13) lays a foundation for Cahn's interpretation and arguments. This foundation consists primarily of the author's attempts to correlate the nine harbingers of Isaiah 9:10 with events of the last decade in America as evidence for the first wave of God's judgment.

In the second part of the book (chapters 14-22), Cahn presents his theory that a second wave of God's judgment, a "second shaking," has taken place as a follow-up to the first. He contends that this is God's final warning of impending severe judgment, which could mean the end of America if the country persists on its present path and refuses to repent.

> [THE PROPHET] "More than one warning may be given," said The Prophet. "If one alarm is ignored, then there comes a second."

> [KAPLAN] "Then there comes a second, or there may come a second?"

> [THE PROPHET] "Then there comes a second."

> [KAPLAN] "Then a second warning is coming?" I asked.

> [THE PROPHET] "A second warning," he said, "a second alarm . . . a second shaking."

> [KAPLAN] "A second shaking of America?"

[KAPLAN] (To GOREN) He turned his gaze so that he was now looking directly into my eyes as he gave his response.

[THE PROPHET] "There comes a second," he said again.[1]

Cahn is certainly correct in his assessment that America is on a path that could lead to its demise. He has rightly enumerated a whole host of sins that have become endemic to the American culture and continue to move the country farther and farther away from many of the moral and ethical foundations on which it was built.

The day may come when God severely judges the United States, and it could even be true that such a judgment is already underway. However, as has been discussed throughout this book, the evidence that Cahn has presented *fails to demonstrate a connection between Isaiah 9:10 and America concerning that judgment*. On careful examination, the case he tries to make for the "Second Shaking" fares no better.

THE MYSTERY AND THE GREAT RECESSION

So, what was the second warning, *the second shaking* to which Cahn refers?

[KAPLAN] "The Prophet spoke of the Harbingers as symbols. That was a clue. The World Trade Center was a symbol of America's global financial and economic power. So what would such a fall foreshadow?"

[GOREN] "An economic . . . fall?"

[KAPLAN] "As in a financial and economic collapse."

[GOREN] "The collapse that began the Great Recession?"

[KAPLAN] "Yes."

[GOREN] "The collapse of the American and global economy is connected to 9/11?"

[KAPLAN] "Yes."[2]

Of course it makes sense that there would be a clear connection between the attacks of 9/11 and subsequent financial and economic problems both nationally and internationally. There is no mystery in that suggestion. However, that is not the issue. The question is whether there is a mystery hidden in *Isaiah 9:10* that connects it to the financial and economic problems of the last decade in the United States and particularly those of the last five years or so. Based on the second half of *The Harbinger*, Cahn's answer, as expected, is a resounding "Yes!" as evidenced by the way the above exchange continues. His belief that Isaiah 9:10 and Israel are deeply connected to recent events in the United States continues to be undeniable:

> [THE PROPHET] "*It all goes back to the prophecy . . . every-thing*—the collapse of Wall Street, the rise and fall of the credit market, the war in Iraq, the collapse of the housing market, the foreclosures, the defaults, the bankruptcies, the government takeovers—everything—politics, foreign policy, world history—everything that happened after. *It all goes back to the prophecy and to the ancient mystery.*"[3]

These claims will be examined in the coming pages.

IT HAD TO HAPPEN...

Any claim that Isaiah 9:10 has been and continues to be fulfilled in America presents serious interpretive problems, as Cahn well knows. That being true, he has insisted that he has been misunderstood by those who think he has suggested anything more than parallels and patterns between Isaiah's prophecy and recent events in America.

Prior to the discussion of the "Second Shaking," however, The Prophet's words once again make it clear that Isaiah's prophecy carries far more meaning and far more force than that of a simple parallel. In Cahn's mind, the passage unquestionably has *prophetic* force because it required certain things to happen. They *had* to happen:

> [THE PROPHET] "So what happens if a warning is given, if the alarms go off, and nobody listens?"

[KAPLAN] "Then it happens."

[THE PROPHET] "So then it happens."

[KAPLAN] "But does it have to happen?" I asked.

[THE PROPHET] "If the warning is rejected, then, yes, it has to happen."[4]

Things that are merely parallels do not necessarily have any connection with one another. They may be connected but they don't have to be. They can involve things that are the same or similar, or they may only have a superficial resemblance to one another. They can be intentional, or they may be entirely coincidental (if anything can be called "coincidental" in view of God's sovereignty).

However, whatever the specific situation may be, there is *no necessary* or *required* relationship between things that are merely parallel to one another. In other words, each thing can exist entirely independently from the others.

On the other hand, prophecy is an entirely different matter. Prophecy involves a *necessary* connection between what is said and a subsequent event. A prophecy and its fulfillment are not independent of one another. If something is prophesied, then something *must* happen—otherwise it has been uttered by a false prophet.

Conversely, if something must happen because of something that was said, then there is a prophetic connection. This is precisely why Cahn cannot legitimately deny that he sees a prophetic connection between Isaiah 9:10 and America. The Prophet said, "If the warning is rejected, then, yes, it has to happen." So, what is it that must happen? The prophesied judgment.

The author has tried to get around this problem by explaining that Isaiah 9:10-11 is merely functioning as a *sign* to America (as noted in chapter 3 of this book). However, if what did happen had to happen, then the sign has prophetic force, and any attempt to distinguish a sign from a prophecy in relation to the Isaiah passage is not convincing.

As the Commentaries Say . . .

A somewhat puzzling feature of *The Harbinger* is the way that Cahn appeals to commentaries numerous times. The following are representative examples:

> [KAPLAN] "I found a match—what The Prophet said to me when he left and what the commentaries said about Isaiah 9:10 . . . they matched."

> [GOREN] "How?"

> [KAPLAN] "In one of the commentaries I found this: '*Divine anger, being a remedial force, will not cease until its purposes are wrought out. . . . Therefore, if . . . Israel resisted one expression of the anger, another must be found.*'"[5]

* * *

> [KAPLAN] "The commentaries were consistent in linking Isaiah 9:10 with the same principle. And then, in another commentary, I found this: '*As the first stage of the judgments has been followed by no true conversion to Jehovah, the Almighty Judge, there comes a second.*'"

Several years ago, a well-known pastor and author of two best-selling books met with some criticism because of the way he seemed to garner biblical support for his ideas. The books sometimes gave the impression that he would hit on an idea and then try to find a biblical passage to support it. Such "proof-texting" is the wrong way to handle the Word of God.

However, a bigger problem was that the author took proof-texting to a new level by extending his search across Bible translations and paraphrases until he found one that best suited a particular point. Even if the majority of accurate translations did not say what he "needed them to say," he could sometimes find a paraphrase that did.

Unfortunately, Jonathan Cahn's selective use of biblical commentaries to support his theories feels remarkably similar. He frequently quotes commentaries that are worded so closely to a particular aspect of his theory that it's not clear whether he has adjusted his wording to match a commentary or found a commentary to match his wording.

In either case, as helpful as commentaries can be, they are not the final word, even though Cahn almost treats them as if they were. Another oddity that compounds the problem of his use of commentaries authoritatively is that *The Prophet* is frequently the one who is quoting the commentaries. Why would a prophet of God need to appeal to commentaries to make, support, or defend his point?

Perhaps Cahn didn't think this through carefully. In the story, The Prophet makes no discernible distinction between the authority of a biblical author and that of a commentator. The impression one gets is that Cahn is using the commentaries almost as if they were inspired by God in some way, as well.

One also senses that Cahn's use of commentaries in this way serves as something of an apologetic for his views. He may be the first to pull all the evidence together in such a way that the hidden ancient mystery is clearly revealed for the first time, but he can also argue that he is not just making this up as he goes—others have also seen and written about these various bits and pieces before.

The result is that this approach helps the author to amass a good number of additional "proofs" for his theories. With this kind of support from historical authorities and biblical scholars, the "coincidences" are just too many and too significant to ignore. This *must* all be from God—or so the reasoning goes.

CHAPTER 12

THE ISAIAH 9:10 EFFECT

THE NEXT major idea that Cahn introduces in connection with the "Second Shaking" is termed the *Isaiah 9:10 Effect*.[1] Just as the theory of the nine harbingers was developed to demonstrate the connection between Isaiah 9:10 and America, the Isaiah 9:10 Effect is crucial to understanding God's second round of warning to America.

> [THE PROPHET] "As in there comes a second, yes. So what would it mean?"
>
> [KAPLAN] "The prophecy has a second part, it leads to something else . . . to a second manifestation."
>
> [THE PROPHET] "The Isaiah 9:10 Effect."
>
> [KAPLAN] "Which is what?"
>
> [THE PROPHET] "This: '*The attempt of a nation to defy the course of its judgment, apart from repentance, will, instead, set in motion a chain of events to bring about the very calamity it sought to avert.*'"

Before going any further, the first question every reader should be asking about The Prophet's definition of the Isaiah 9:10 Effect is, "Where did this definition come from?" It certainly didn't come from Isaiah 9:10. Neither did it come from any of the verses in the vicinity of Isaiah 9:10. The importance of this matter cannot be overstated because the rest of Cahn's entire theory depends on *this* theory—that there really is such a thing as the Isaiah 9:10 Effect. This is immediately apparent as the dialogue continues:

> [KAPLAN] "And this all has to do with America?" I asked.

> [THE PROPHET] "Seven years after 9/11," he said, "the American economy collapsed, triggering a global economic implosion. Behind it all, and all that followed, was something much deeper than economics."

> [KAPLAN] "Behind the collapse of Wall Street and the American economy was . . ."

> [THE PROPHET] "Isaiah 9:10."[2]

In the author's mind, Isaiah's words in the alleged Isaiah 9:10 Effect actually *cause things to happen*. This is clearly affirmed in the following exchange at the end of chapter 16:

> [KAPLAN] "As in the Isaiah 9:10 Effect?"

> [THE PROPHET] "Yes, but in this mystery the connections are even more beyond the realm of the natural."

> [KAPLAN] "They're supernatural?"

> [THE PROPHET] "You could say that."

> [KAPLAN] "And they connect 9/11 to the economic collapse?"

> [THE PROPHET] "Not only do they connect them . . . *they determined them . . . down to the time each would take place.*"

> [KAPLAN] "An ancient mystery?"

> [THE PROPHET] "Yes, an ancient mystery upon which the global economy and every transaction within *it was determined, a mystery that begins more than three thousand years ago in the sands of a Middle Eastern desert.*"

A Fatal Flaw in the Theory

So, the question remains, "Where does the concept of the Isaiah 9:10 Effect come from?" Since it doesn't come from the text itself nor from the immediate context, nor is anything remotely similar to the Isaiah 9:10 Effect mentioned or implied anywhere else in Scripture, it appears to be just another one of those things in the book that has been made up. Yet one would never guess that from reading *The Harbinger*. Cahn presents the Isaiah 9:10 Effect as if it were an inviolable scriptural principle—that once it is set in motion, the corresponding prescribed outcome is inevitable.

However, even if he were discussing only the fulfillment of Isaiah 9:10 in ancient Israel, this would not be a good way to explain how prophecies work. The reason that prophesied events happen is because *God* causes them to happen, not because the *prophecy itself* somehow causes them to happen. Yet Cahn seems to be suggesting that as a principle the Isaiah 9:10 Effect can *cause* these same events to happen anywhere at any time once it is triggered.

Of course, if it were simply a general principle such as that of "sowing and reaping," or like the many principles found in Proverbs, it wouldn't necessarily be as problematic. Even this would disregard the fact that Isaiah 9:10 does not appear to be a principle in context. The Isaiah 9:10 Effect is presented as being so specific that it is independently formulaic. In other words, if and when the First Harbinger happens, then it is just a short matter of time until the Second Harbinger also happens—which will then be followed by each of the other harbingers—until finally the judgment takes place.

As noted before, Cahn strenuously argues that he has been misunderstood by those who believe he is saying that Isaiah 9:10 specifically applies to America. However, if that is not what he is saying, then the only other possible explanation is that the Isaiah 9:10 Effect is an independent and formulaic principle that operates in a mystical way through the power of the words themselves. Once again, he tries to have it both ways, as can be seen in the necessary results of the Isaiah 9:10 Effect (emphasis added):

- "So the rebuilding *must* begin . . ."[3]
- "So the Gazit Stone *must* be brought . . ."[4]
- "...the Sycamore *must* be replaced . . ."[5]
- "The Erez Tree *must* be planted . . ."[6]
- "The vow *must* be spoken . . ."[7]
- "But according to the Isaiah 9:10 Effect the second calamity *must* be born out effectively of the first . . ."[8]

This leaves Cahn with two major problems. If Isaiah 9:10 is to both ancient Israel and America, he is faced with an insurmountable hermeneutical problem. But if instead there really is such a thing as the Isaiah 9:10 Effect, he then has a historical problem.

What if "the breach" and "the terrorist" had been observed in 1812 or 1861 or 1941? In theory, could someone have discovered the "hidden ancient mystery" of Isaiah 9:10 in 1949? And if it had been claimed that Pearl Harbor was a breach by an enemy who persistently used terrorist tactics throughout the war in the Pacific (which the Japanese did), then could it not be argued that God's hedge of protection had been withdrawn prior to December 7, 1941? And if the hedge of protection had been removed long before 9/11, had God put yet another hedge of protection in place since WWII? The questions are truly endless.

This is not an attempt to mock the author. This is a very serious issue because if he is correct about the Isaiah 9:10 Effect, then it could have happened at any time in the past or it could happen again at any time in the future. On the other hand, if it could only have happened one time on September 11, 2001, then *there is no such thing as the Isaiah 9:10 Effect as a principle.*

OTHER ". . . EFFECT" PASSAGES?

If Cahn is right about the Isaiah 9:10 Effect, this raises another very important question: Are there any other prophetic passages in the Old Testament that also function like the *Isaiah 9:10 Effect*? How many other prophecies that were directed to Israel can also be correlated to historical events in the United States?

Is there also a "Genesis 12:2 Effect?":

I will make you a great nation; I will bless you and make your name great; and you shall be a blessing.

Or a "Joshua 1:2 Effect?":

Every place that the sole of your foot will tread upon I have given you, as I said to Moses.

Are there *dozens* of others? Or is Isaiah 9:10 the *only* such passage in the entire Bible? If the Isaiah 9:10 Effect really exists, then it seems remarkably unlikely that it would be the only such principle in the entire Old Testament. But if not from the context, how could it possibly be known whether any given passage is supposed to function in this way? And yet there is nothing whatsoever in the context of Isaiah 9:10 that would suggest the existence of such an effect.

As noted earlier: *If a proposed theological or spiritual idea is not found in the Bible, or if it cannot at least be supported by the text in some way, then someone made it up.* This is exactly the nature of the Isaiah 9:10 Effect—someone made it up.

CHAPTER 13

THE FINANCIAL COLLAPSE

THE VERY CONCEPT of the Isaiah 9:10 Effect itself is problematic, and Cahn's attempt to demonstrate how it actually played out in practical terms is confusing and enigmatic. He engages in making even larger leaps of logic, putting the story on a trajectory that takes it further than ever from Scripture and in some cases into the ethereal realm of allegory:

[KAPLAN] "Behind the collapse of Wall Street and the American economy was . . ."

[THE PROPHET] *"Isaiah 9:10."*

[KAPLAN] "How?"

[THE PROPHET] ". . . according to the *Isaiah 9:10 Effect,* the second calamity must be effectively born out of the first . . . and out of the nation's response to that first calamity."

[KAPLAN] "So then the collapse of the economy and Wall Street would have to somehow go back to 9/11."[1]

* * *

[KAPLAN] "And it all would lead up to the economic collapse?"

[THE PROPHET] "In part," he said. "And for all that, it would be yet another manifestation of the *Isaiah 9:10 Effect that would bring about the collapse of the American and global economy.* And this too was born out of the ruins of 9/11. The most critical effect of the calamity on the American and global economy would begin six days after the attack."

[KAPLAN] "As a response to the calamity?"

[THE PROPHET] "Yes," he said, "as in the ancient vow. . . ."[2]

In this exchange Cahn directly ties America's economic collapse to the statement by America's leaders that "we will rebuild." This in turn is connected to what he claims[3] is a vow in Isaiah 9:10. Once again, it is impossible to accept that he is arguing for simply a parallel or pattern. He makes a *direct prophetic connection* between ancient Israel and the United States. However, Cahn takes this part of his theory far beyond the rebuilding that was prophesied in Isaiah into an elaborate maze of national economic policies, corporate stock exchanges, and international financial markets.

AN ALLEGORICAL BLUNDER

In an attempt to bridge the logical gap that he has created between the biblical text and current events, Cahn introduces allegory into the interpretive equation—a decision that was doomed from the outset.

[KAPLAN] "So what happened six days after the attack?"

[THE PROPHET] "*The Isaiah 9:10 Effect begins* with the nation's response to the first calamity."

[KAPLAN] "So the effect would begin with the proclaiming of the vow on Capitol Hill, the next day."

[THE PROPHET] "Yes," said The Prophet, "but those were words, 'We will rebuild.' It would be the following Monday that those words would be translated into reality. It was the day that the Federal Reserve attempted to inject liquidity into the market in a campaign to avert economic disaster and ensure that America would indeed rebuild and recover."

[KAPLAN] "As ancient Israel had attempted to defy the consequences of its first calamity."

[THE PROPHET] "*Yes, except that the hewn stones of America's recovery were primarily economic.* So on the first Monday after 9/11, the Federal Reserve slashed its target interest rate still further . . . as the first concrete act of the nation's rebuilding."[4]

The hewn stones of America were primarily economic? Where does Isaiah 9 suggest that the hewn stones carried an allegorical or metaphorical meaning beyond the literal meaning? It's one thing to say that rebuilding has economic implications. But to say that the *meaning* of *hewn stones* is rebuilding the financial foundations or that they are symbolic of economic recovery lacks any textual support and is therefore completely unbiblical.

Cahn's imposition of his own ideas on the text represents a serious departure from a literal, grammatical, historical hermeneutic. Yet he states the supposed underlying meaning so matter-of-factly and with such confidence that he appears to simply assume that the reader will accept his allegorical interpretation of historical events without giving it a second thought.

A complex and tedious analysis

The story continues with a discussion of slashing interest rates by the Federal Reserve, which would be so extreme that it "would open up an era of easy money."[5] Cahn then delves into a complex and rather tedious discussion of the economic ins and outs of the Federal Reserve, the U.S. Treasury, the global economy, interest rates, monetary policy, credit bubbles, housing booms, the stock market, and more.

A significant amount of time and effort would be required to even begin to evaluate the accuracy of the many components of the author's analysis. Undoubtedly Cahn has done a lot of research into this matter, and he does include footnotes to support some (though certainly not all) of his statements.

However, he has ventured into an area that involves such highly interpretive, speculative, and often subjective analyses that even respected economists and financial experts will seldom agree on all of the causes and effects for these types of things. Cahn's attempt to prove a biblical connection and precise prophetic fulfillment with this argument is less than convincing.

The following are just two of many examples where the author makes far-reaching claims with no reference to supporting research and evidence:

> [THE PROPHET] *"Easier mortgages* would cause an already rising housing market to explode beyond all standard *economic fundamentals*, creating an unprecedented *housing and building boom.* The exploding housing market would *lead homeowners*

to borrow and spend against the rising value of their homes. The phenomenon would create *credit bubbles throughout the economy.* This, in turn, would encourage *massive inflows of capital from Asia* to compound the problem. The stock market would surge along with the *volume of monies borrowed and leveraged.* And the effect would spread *throughout the world.*"[6]

* * *

[THE PROPHET] "In September of 2008, the American financial system began to implode, triggering the greatest economic disaster since the Great Depression. The American-led global economic explosion turned into an American-led global economic implosion. The house of cards was collapsing and drawing the world into its fall. *And so behind the entire global economic collapse . . . was Isaiah 9:10.* It all began in the ruins of 9/11."[7]

At the risk of beating the proverbial "dead horse," it bears repeating that despite the author's strong denials that he sees a direct connection between Isaiah 9:10, ancient Israel, and post-9/11 America, here he has linked them once again. However, now the connection for which Cahn is arguing extends beyond the 9/11 attacks to include the ongoing economic crisis in the U.S. since September 2008. Then he goes even further by not only linking America with the ancient mystery of Isaiah, but he also proposes that the entire world is directly affected and that this, too, is part of Isaiah's hidden message:

[THE PROPHET] "And notice, Nouriel, the dynamic keeps getting larger. It begins with the voicing of the ancient vow. Then it becomes a direction, then the policy of an entire nation, and *then a collapse affecting the course of the entire world.* The Harbingers draw in everything to themselves, from the Federal Reserve to the global economy . . . . *They touch the entire world, and no one realizes that it's all part of the ancient mystery.*"[8]

Cahn has continued his foray into the speculative unknown and strays further and further from the biblical text. Although Isaiah 9:10 involves a very localized regional conflict, Cahn has made its contemporary fulfillment a global matter.

Where do his conclusions come from? Certainly not from Isaiah 9:10, nor from any of the surrounding context. Unfortunately, though not surprisingly, he has again turned to commentaries for support. This time, however, a commentary is not used to support the Bible *per se* but to link an analysis of the current economic crisis to both Isaiah 9:10 and September 11, 2001:

> [KAPLAN] "Isaiah 9:10 translated into modern economics."

> [THE PROPHET] "Exactly. And from another source: 'The financial house of cards was slowly built following the 9/11 attacks. As the U.S. government tried to revive the economy by repeatedly dropping interest rates, families lunged at the opportunity to refinance their mortgages. Now, the collapse of the mortgage market is felt around the world.'"

> [KAPLAN] "'*Divine anger*,' I said, quoting what I had read, '*being a remedial force, will not cease until its purposes are wrought out. . . . If one expression is resisted another must be found.*'"

> [THE PROPHET] "And where did you get that?" he asked.

> [KAPLAN] "From a commentary on Isaiah 9:10."

> [THE PROPHET] "Very good, Nouriel. So you've been searching."[9]

EXPOSING THE FOUNDATION

Cahn introduces the next aspect of his financial collapse theory by predictably merging Israel and America as objects of Isaiah's prophecy and the mystery hidden therein:

> [KAPLAN] "You're giving me the seal of the Sixth Harbinger."

> [THE PROPHET] "That's correct."

> [KAPLAN] "The fallen Sycamore . . . the tree of Israel's judgment."

[THE PROPHET] "And why am I giving it to you a second time?" he asked.

[KAPLAN] "Because it has something to do with the second shaking."

[THE PROPHET] "It does," he said. "But also for another reason."

[KAPLAN] "What?"

[THE PROPHET] "Within the Sycamore are two mysteries—one going back to the last days of ancient Israel, and the other going back to the first days . . . "

[KAPLAN] "The first days of ancient Israel?"

[THE PROPHET] "The first days of America."

More misleading "support"

In this section of *The Harbinger*, Cahn continues to try to build additional support for his theory by reintroducing "The Sycamore," which is the Sixth Harbinger. He quotes prophecies by Ezekiel and Jeremiah while explaining them in such a way that the reader would think they are referring to the same events as Isaiah and at the same time giving further insight into the mystery concerning America.

Ezekiel 13:14—

So I will break down the wall you have plastered with untempered mortar, and bring it down to the ground, so that its foundation will be uncovered; it will fall, and you shall be consumed in the midst of it. Then you shall know that I am the LORD.

Jeremiah 45:4—

Thus you shall say to him, "Thus says the LORD: 'Behold, what I have built I will break down, and what I have planted I will pluck up.'"

The first problem is that neither Ezekiel nor Jeremiah were referring to the Assyrian attacks on the Northern Kingdom of Israel, as was Isaiah. Rather, both were prophesying over 100 years *after* the destruction of the Northern Kingdom, and thus they were focused on what was left of Israel in the Southern Kingdom of Judah. This would not necessarily be a serious problem were it not for the fact that Cahn repeatedly does this type of thing—misleading the reader by giving details that appear to fit and support his case, while leaving out other details that could weaken or even contradict it.

Beyond this, of course, similarities can be found between many different judgments in the Bible, including those that are not connected with each other in any way. This is particularly true when the judgment involves a foreign power launching a military assault. Even the most basic of military strategies involves breaching defenses at their weakest point and then systematically dismantling them—that is, tearing down walls to their foundations. Unfortunately, Cahn uses just these sorts of similarities again and again to overwhelm the reader with volumes of corroborating evidence. This is misleading.

Even more significant than these issues is the fact that Cahn has completely missed the primary point of the passages in both Ezekiel and Jeremiah. He compounds the problem by *wrongly allegorizing* what is said in Ezekiel but then oddly missing what is a *metaphor* in Jeremiah.

Mishandling Ezekiel 13

The passage in Ezekiel is not so much a prophecy about an actual military attack against Israel (although it does include that). Rather, it is primarily an oracle against the false prophets who have been telling the people that they have nothing to worry about—that God will not bring judgment upon them. Ezekiel figuratively (which is different from allegory) speaks of their false prophecies as "untempered mortar" (13:11,14) that provides no protection for walls made of clay bricks when hit by storms packing strong winds and torrential rains. In other words, the assurances of peace and safety given by the false prophets will be shown to be lies that offer no protection against God's judgment when they see the walls of the city torn down to their foundations. Ezekiel is making a different point than Isaiah did in chapter 9, even though Isaiah speaks of false prophets in verse 15.

Furthermore, when the Lord speaks about the walls being torn down so that the foundations are uncovered, He is not speaking figuratively, as Cahn argues. The Lord is saying that when the literal physical foundations are exposed, the people will then understand that they have believed false prophets. Cahn wrongly turns the Lord's words into an allegory and then uses that allegory as a springboard for launching into another speculative theory in the rest of the chapter.

> [THE PROPHET] "Its foundation will be uncovered. What foundations do you think the prophecy is referring to, Nouriel?"
>
> [KAPLAN] "The foundation of a wall, it would seem."
>
> [THE PROPHET] "A foundation is that upon which something stands or rests or is built. So a nation's foundation is that upon which it stands . . . or on which it was founded . . . or that in which it rests or places its trust. The nations of the ancient world trusted in their idols and gods. Modern nations trust in their powers, their militaries, their economies, their resources. But what it's saying here is that in the days of judgment a nation's foundations are laid bare. Its idols fall, and its powers fail. It's one of the key signs of judgment—the laying bare of foundations."

Cahn's elaborate allegorization of the Lord's words is completely without biblical warrant. The problem is not that he is wrong about nations misplacing their trust in everything but God. Of course Cahn is right about that. The problem is that he states that this is what the passage in *Ezekiel* is about. It is not. The Word of God cannot be manipulated and misused in this way.

Mishandling Jeremiah 45

The way that Cahn handles the Jeremiah passage makes one sense that perhaps a bit of interpretive sleight-of-hand is going on once again. In this case, he gives the impression that the phrase "what I have planted I will pluck up" in Jeremiah can be directly correlated with the statement that "the sycamores have been cut down" in Isaiah. The reader would therefore assume that Jeremiah was talking about sycamore trees being plucked up. In fact, he was not.

> [THE PROPHET] "But in the days of Israel's judgment, that which was built up would be broken down and that which was planted would be uprooted. Two images of national judgment—the breaking down and the uprooting."

> [KAPLAN] "Repeat that," I said.

> [THE PROPHET] "Repeat what?" he asked.

> [KAPLAN] "Jeremiah's prophecy."

> [THE PROPHET] "'Behold, what I have built I will break down.'"

> [KAPLAN] "'The bricks have fallen,'" I answered.

> [THE PROPHET] "'*And what I have planted I will pluck up.*'"

> [KAPLAN] "'*The sycamores have been cut down,*'" I answered.

> [THE PROPHET] "Yes, Nouriel, it follows the same pattern."

> [KAPLAN] "It's the same pattern and the same order as Isaiah 9:10. First comes the breaking down—the fallen bricks. *Then comes the uprooting—the sycamore.*"[10]

Once again, this is very misleading. Unless the reader took the time to actually look at the Jeremiah passage in the Bible, he would never know that *Cahn did not quote the entire verse.* If he had, it would have been obvious that the claimed precise link between Jeremiah 45:4 and Isaiah 9:10 does not exist.

Jeremiah 45:4—

> Thus you shall say to him, "Thus says the Lord: 'Behold, what I have built I will break down, and what I have planted I will pluck up, that is, this whole land.'"

What is "plucked up" is not sycamores. Rather it is the nation itself, with no reference to trees whatsoever. Even this would not necessarily have to be a significant problem because both have to do with Israel's destruction. However, because of the way Cahn argues for such a high level of precision in the corresponding details between the two passages, this omission is notably problematic. Leaving out the last phrase in Jeremiah 45:4 is not being at all forthright with the reader about the passage.

Mishandling the details

Another interpretive and practical issue is that Cahn mixes and exchanges elements of the prophecies and historical events. In Isaiah 9:10, the fact of the sycamores being cut down obviously has nothing to do with the foundations of the city. There is no connection between them whatsoever, either physically or logically.

However, in a new allegorical twist, using tortuous logic, Cahn tries to apply Isaiah's prophecy to the United States by connecting the sycamores to the foundation of America's economy, which he says is the New York Stock Exchange. Thus the NYSE is the foundation of America's power as a nation. The author then attempts to connect everything together through what is known as the "Buttonwood Agreement":

> [THE PROPHET] "In March of 1792, a secret meeting took place at a Manhattan hotel . . . the merchants again gathered together, this time at 68 Wall Street to sign a document. . . . The document was called the *Buttonwood Agreement*. The organization born of the agreement would be known as the *Buttonwood Association* and later as the *New York Stock and Exchange Board*, and finally as the *New York Stock Exchange*."

* * *

> [THE PROPHET] "The twenty-four merchants used to meet and carry on their transactions under a buttonwood tree that grew on Wall Street . . ."

* * *

> [THE PROPHET] "*Buttonwood*," he said, "is, in essence, just another way of saying *sycamore* . . ."

* * *

[KAPLAN] "And the New York Stock Exchange is, in essence, the Sycamore Association."

* * *

[THE PROPHET] "The World Trade Center was a towering symbol of what that power had become. But the sycamore was the symbol of its origin."

[KAPLAN] "The foundation," I said, "the foundation of a nation's power."[11]

Therefore, when the sycamore at Ground Zero was blown over and uprooted, Cahn contends that this was *symbolic* of America's foundation being exposed. And herein lies the problem. As noted earlier, signs from God carry prophetic significance. They are revelatory.

Likewise, symbols signify something—they are signs. Because of this fact, something can be a biblical symbol only if God intends for it to have that function. Thus Cahn essentially assigns biblical symbolic status to the Ground Zero sycamore because he believes that it is directly tied to both the ancient mystery of Isaiah 9:10 and to America's financial collapse:

[KAPLAN] "So the Sycamore wasn't only a warning of judgment; it was, at the same time, a specific foreshadow of economic collapse."

[THE PROPHET] "The striking down of the sycamore tree is a biblical sign of judgment," he said. "But the same tree is also a symbol specific to American power."

[KAPLAN] "So then the uprooting of the sycamore would foreshadow . . ."

[THE PROPHET] "Yes," he said, "it would foreshadow the uprooting of America's financial and economic power."[12]

Just when it seems that Cahn has stretched things as far as he possibly can, he goes even further by turning the entire life cycle of the Ground-Zero sycamore into an allegory, a metaphor for the rise and fall of America as a world power:

[KAPLAN] "So what does it mean?" I asked. "What does it mean specifically for America?"

[THE PROPHET] "If a living sycamore signifies the rise of America as the world's preeminent financial power, what then does an uprooted sycamore signify?"

[KAPLAN] "Its fall," I answered. "It would have to signify its fall."

[THE PROPHET] "God had allowed America's power to be planted here, to take root, to grow, and to branch out over the world. The nation would rise to unprecedented heights of global power and economic prosperity. But in its departure and its rejection of His ways, a sign was given. If now it refused to turn back, the blessings and prosperity symbolized by the sycamore would be removed—that which had been built up would be broken down, and that which had been planted would be uprooted."[13]

The Seventh Harbinger revisited

Cahn has now set the stage for reintroducing the Seventh Harbinger, *The Erez Tree*:

[KAPLAN] "And they connect 9/11 to the economic collapse?"

[THE PROPHET] "Not only do they connect them . . . they determined them . . . down to the time each would take place."

[KAPLAN] "An ancient mystery?"

[THE PROPHET] "Yes, an ancient mystery upon which the global economy and every transaction within it was determined, a mystery that begins more than three thousand years ago in the sands of a Middle Eastern desert."[14]

Just as the Ground Zero sycamore was also assigned a symbolic meaning, the Erez tree is no longer only a literal Norway spruce. It now becomes symbolic and is connected with the next phase of God's judgment against America and the world—the Shemitah.

CHAPTER 14

THE SHEMITAH

AS HAS BEEN SHOWN repeatedly, despite Cahn's claims to the contrary, *The Harbinger* very clearly and directly connects America and ancient Israel through Isaiah's prophecy. In chapter 17 of his book, however, Cahn goes well beyond this and turns to a theme that casts America into a role and situation that was exclusively reserved for Israel. Cahn believes that he has discovered another mystery in addition to the one hidden in Isaiah 9:10—the mystery of the *Shemitah* (Hebrew for *release*)—and that this mystery is now affecting the United States.

> [KAPLAN] "I still don't see how it connects with America."

> [THE PROPHET] "Behind the collapse of Wall Street and the implosion of the American and world economy, behind all of it lies the mystery of the Shemitah."[1]

Later The Prophet explains:

> [THE PROPHET] "In the days of the prophet Jeremiah, with Jerusalem lying in ruins and the people taken away in captivity, the key that held *the timing of the nation's judgment was hidden in the mystery of the Shemitah.*"[2]

Cahn's argument builds on the fact that two stockmarket crashes occurred on exactly the last day of the Shemitah year according to the Jewish calendar in both 2001 and 2008. Without a doubt, this is an interesting phenomenon (and will be discussed later). However, for now, suffice it to say that this is where any similarity to the Shemitah required of Israel begins and ends.

THE SHEMITAH AND ISRAEL

Just as Israel was to observe the seventh day of the week, the Sabbath, as a day of rest, they were also to observe the seventh year, the Shemitah, as a year of rest. The Shemitah was a sabbath year. In the Law of Moses, God had commanded that every seventh year Israel must allow the land to completely rest, with no harvesting, reaping, or any other work in the fields. In addition, all who owed money to creditors were to be released from their debts.

Deuteronomy 15:1–2—

At the end of every seven years you shall grant a release of debts. And this is the form of the release: Every creditor who has lent anything to his neighbor shall release it; he shall not require it of his neighbor or his brother, because it is called the LORD's release.

Humanly speaking, this law has "economic disaster" written all over it. How could a nation possibly survive such an economic requirement every seventh year? The Shemitah would almost certainly cripple any nation attempting to practice it.

However, Israel was not just any nation. It was the one and only nation chosen by God to be His covenant people. Israel was separate and distinct from all other nations and was called to be uniquely faithful to and dependent on Him.

God would demonstrate His love and faithfulness to Israel by providing enough in the sixth year to meet the nation's needs the following year. In fact, the land would actually yield three year's worth of produce in the sixth year (Leviticus 25:20-21). Conversely, Israel would demonstrate her faith in God both as a nation and as individuals by obeying His command to keep the Shemitah and trusting Him for the results.

The word *shemitah* in its noun form is found five times in the Old Testament and only in Deuteronomy. The verb form appears nine times, and except for once in Exodus, it too is found only in Deuteronomy.

The concept (though not the word) also appears in Leviticus 25:3-4—

Six years you shall sow your field, and six years you shall prune your vineyard, and gather its fruit; but in the seventh year there shall be a sabbath of solemn rest for the land, a sabbath to the LORD. You shall neither sow your field nor prune your vineyard.

Then after every seventh Shemitah year (i.e., after 49 years) there was to be an additional "Jubilee Year."

Leviticus 25:10–11—

And you shall consecrate the fiftieth year, and proclaim liberty throughout all the land to all its inhabitants. It shall be a Jubilee for you; and each of you shall return to his possession, and each of you shall return to his family. That fiftieth year shall be a Jubilee to you; in it you shall neither sow nor reap what grows of its own accord, nor gather the grapes of your untended vine.

In the next chapter, the Lord warned of multiple waves of horrific judgments that will fall on the nation if they fail to keep His commandments, including His sabbaths. If, after all that, Israel still refuses to repent and return to the Lord in response to these judgments, He warned of what was to come, which was essentially an imposed Shemitah:

Leviticus 26:33–35—

I will scatter you among the nations and draw out a sword after you; your land shall be desolate and your cities waste. Then the land shall enjoy its sabbaths as long as it lies desolate and you are in your enemies' land; then the land shall rest and enjoy its sabbaths. As long as it lies desolate it shall rest— for the time it did not rest on your sabbaths when you dwelt in it.

Hundreds of years later, Israel experienced precisely this judgment— first with the Assyrian invasion and later with the Babylonian invasion, conquest, and captivity. Because Judah had not observed the Shemitah for seventy cycles of seven years, the nation was in captivity (thus leaving the land idle) for seventy years.

The nation had not observed the Shemitah because they had forsaken their God, had intermarried with foreign women, and were worshiping their pagan gods. Therefore God imposed a Shemitah upon Israel as a judgment rather than a blessing because they had failed to observe the Shemitah willingly.

There were certainly many other judgments against both Israel and Judah because of persistent lack of faith in the God of Israel and their blatant worship of other gods, with all of the attendant pagan practices. There were attacks and wars, storms and droughts, sickness and plagues, corrupt kings and wicked priests.

However, the Bible connects *none* of those to the Shemitah. The Shemitah that God imposed as a judgment was very specific and involved *only the nation of Israel*. No Gentile nations were ever obligated to keep the Shemitah, and in the absence of this obligation, there is no scriptural basis for suggesting that any Gentile nation would ever experience an imposed Shemitah judgment.

The Shemitah as a Mystery

God defined the Shemitah very explicitly, and the Scriptures make it abundantly clear how it was to function in Israel and the consequences associated with failure to observe it. Obviously, there was no *mystery* concerning the Shemitah and the nation of Israel.

As he has done before, Cahn introduces a concept that has no scriptural support. He does, however, correctly present the fact that the Shemitah was never given to nor binding upon any nation other than Israel:

> [KAPLAN] "But what does it have to do with America? America has never had a Sabbath Year."

> [THE PROPHET] "That's correct. It was only commanded for one nation. But the issue here isn't the literal observance of the Shemitah or any requirement to keep it."[3]

Yet he wrongly makes the case that the Shemitah is essentially a universal, inviolable *principle* that functions much like the Isaiah 9:10 Effect. Consequently, the mystery of the Shemitah, which the author has somehow discovered, *can* directly affect America.

> [KAPLAN] "Then what is the issue here?" I asked.

> [THE PROPHET] "The issue here," he replied, "is its dynamic, its effect, and its consequence."[4]

By explaining it this way, Cahn tries to make it appear as if the Shemitah is somehow mysteriously integrated into the order of the universe and that it operates both nationally and internationally. Furthermore, he incorporates this idea into his financial collapse theory and actually builds the entire theory around this view of the Shemitah.

However, just as with the Isaiah 9:10 Effect, Scripture nowhere presents the Shemitah as a universal principle or pattern connected with God's judgment. The Shemitah was anything but a mystery. And because of the way that Cahn tries to make the case for the "mystery of the Shemitah," it represents one of the most thoroughly unbiblical ideas in the entire book, and his argument for it also includes some of the most misleading "support."

THE SHEMITAH AS A PRINCIPLE

To lay a foundation for the argument that the Shemitah is a universal principle, Cahn makes the following assertion through the words of Nouriel Kaplan:

> [KAPLAN] "Seven years—the biblical period of time that concerns a nation's financial and economic realms."[5]

Although it is true that Israel was on a seven-year economic cycle imposed by God as part of the Law of Moses, this was not true of any Gentile nation. Nor are there any biblical passages to support the idea suggested by Kaplan in the story that seven years represent a natural economic cycle for nations in general.

Furthermore, extensive internet research does not reveal any uniform conventional wisdom or consensus among economists or financial experts that seven years is a known natural economic or financial cycle. Things are said about various cycles that range from three to ten years, and a couple of people have *suggested* seven, but cycles of even roughly seven years apparently do not exist. The biblical Shemitah, however, was exactly *seven years to the day*.

Cahn's theory that the Shemitah is a universal principle is yet another example of speculation raised to the level of fact. Yet the second half of the book is built almost entirely on this theory.

THE SHEMITAH AS A SIGN

Cahn takes this unscriptural theory even further by proposing that the Shemitah is a sign—not just to Israel, but to any nation.

[KAPLAN] "And what does that mean?"

[THE PROPHET] "The issue is the Shemitah as a sign."

[KAPLAN] "The Shemitah as a sign . . . ?"

[THE PROPHET] "The sign of the Shemitah, given to a nation that has driven God out of its life and replaced Him with idols and the pursuit of gain. The issue is the Shemitah as a sign of judgment, the sign that specifically touches a nation's financial and economic realms."[6]

If the Shemitah is a sign, this means that it is a predictor of things to come. It must be revelatory, as are all signs. In other words, if God warns that a specific judgment is on its way because of failure to observe the Shemitah and that this judgment will be executed through a specific set of events, then when those events begin to happen they reveal that the judgment has begun. However, in the absence of such a prophetic warning, even if identical events happen, it cannot be concluded with any certainty that God is executing a Shemitah or Shemitah-type judgment against America.

As noted earlier, just because God judged Egypt through a plague of locusts, another such plague somewhere, even in Egypt, does not necessarily mean that God is specifically judging those people. Although God judged ancient Israel through a severe drought in the time of Elijah,[7] this does not mean that the present drought of 2012 in much of the United States is the result of God's judgment. Of course, it could be, but the Creation is under the curse of the Fall, and terrible things happen in nature apart from God's miraculous intervention. Not only does the rain fall on the just and the unjust, but *both* can also experience natural disasters.

Because the Word of God does not give the required prophetic warning concerning America and the Shemitah, there is no scriptural basis to interpret recent events as a sign that God is imposing a Shemitah judgment on the United States. Even if it is true that America is in the very midst of God's judgment, it cannot be said biblically that any *signs* point to the judgment being related to the Shemitah—that is unless something is going on that Cahn has repeatedly denied.

THE SHEMITAH AND AMERICA

What, then, could bring someone to suggest any sort of connection between the Shemitah and America? The only potential explanation would seem to be that Cahn believes that the founders were right about America being in covenant with God—if not as a new Israel as such, then at least as one patterned after Israel's covenantal relationship with Him. This is not to suggest that Cahn believes that national Israel has been replaced and has no future in God's program. He has said that he does not believe this. Unfortunately, there seems to be a significant disconnect between what the author says he believes about this and the ideas he so clearly presents in *The Harbinger*.

THE CASE FOR THE SHEMITAH

The examples Cahn uses to demonstrate that America is going through an imposed Shemitah feel contrived. In contrast, the Shemitah in ancient Israel was simple: The Israelites were not to work the land, and the wealthy lenders were required to forgive the debts owed to them by average people.

Later, when Israel fell into sin, God *imposed* the Shemitah on Israel, forcing them to stop working the land completely by taking the nation into captivity. And, as captives, the wealthy were brought down to the level of their debtors, and the financial system *completely* collapsed. The imposed Shemitah was not simply a sign—it was the judgment itself. It meant utter devastation. Almost everyone lost almost everything.

Since the situation with America has not come close to approaching this level of disaster, Cahn must go to great lengths to support his interpretation of both the Bible and history. He has clearly done extensive research and has assembled an impressive array of facts and figures. Because he writes and speaks with conviction and authority, he makes a case that initially seems compelling—and one that has persuaded a lot of people that he is right.

The "fallow land"

As noted, the first major component of the imposed Shemitah was that the Lord forced Israel to allow the land to lie completely fallow by having much of the nation carried away into captivity—there was no one to work the land. However, in America there has been no collapse of the agricultural sector nor any other sectors that might be considered modern-day economic equivalents. There is no parallel to one of the most important aspects of the imposed Shemitah and nothing to indicate that an imposed Shemitah might be underway. The Shemitah *cannot be found*.

Fannie Mae and Freddie Mac

An analysis of the other major component, concerning credit and debt, reveals that the parallels proposed by the author are not much closer. Cahn draws his support almost exclusively from the failure of a few large financial institutions and the response of the federal government. He cites four major corporations: Fannie Mae, Freddie Mac, Lehman Brothers, and AIG.

> [THE PROPHET] "Each failure, each remission, each Shemitah triggers the next and the next as the global economy continues disintegrating. Then, in late August, early September, as the year of Shemitah enters its last and climactic phase, so too does the financial crisis."

> [KAPLAN] "With the collapse of Fannie Mae and Freddie Mac."

> [THE PROPHET] "Yes," he said, "and then of Lehman Brothers, and then of the global economy—everything reaching the climax on September 29, 2008, the last and climactic day of the Shemitah."

> [KAPLAN] "Everything following the ancient pattern."[8]

Although these events were significant factors in the economic crisis of 2008, including the stock market, this does not follow "the ancient pattern"—not at all. The ancient pattern was that Israel was invaded and overrun by a foreign army with everything of value either destroyed or carried away. In sharp contrast, America suffered one relatively minor attack. (Perhaps it seems almost sacrilegious to call 9/11 a minor attack, but compared to what ancient Israel endured, it really was minor.)

And even though the U.S. and global economies have gone through a serious contraction (in the business sense), and certainly many people have been hurt financially, it has not even come close to the scale, especially in relative terms, of the utter devastation that occurred in Israel. Even Cahn himself rightly notes that Fannie Mae and Freddie Mac were rescued by the federal government when the Federal Financial Housing Authority placed them under conservatorship.

Not only did they not collapse, but according to an August 2010 article on ProblemBankList.com:

> Fannie and Freddie are not likely to disappear anytime soon. The combined mortgage giants, now 80% owned by the government, *continue to provide approximately 75% of funding to the mortgage market.* In addition, Fannie and Freddie insure or own $5.7 trillion of the outstanding total of $11 trillion in mortgages. *The government has agreed to provide unlimited funding* while policy makers debate how to reform the mortgage system to prevent Fannie and Freddie from again becoming a systemic risk to the financial system.[9]

The financial woes of Fannie Mae and Freddie Mac cannot be compared with what Israel suffered—and they definitely were not symptomatic of an imposed Shemitah.

Lehman Brothers

Then there is the matter of Lehman Brothers. It is true that when Lehman Brothers filed the largest bankruptcy in history after being denied a federal bailout, the U.S. and world markets were rattled for weeks. However, Cahn's analysis is filled with overstatements that don't reflect the reality of what happened:

> [THE PROPHET] "Lehman Brothers filed for bankruptcy—the largest bankruptcy in American history up to that date. It would be called the collapse heard around the world. The fall of Lehman Brothers would, in turn, trigger the collapse of Wall Street and the global financial implosion."[10]

However, Wall Street did not collapse, and the global economy did not implode. They were seriously shocked, even damaged, but they did not collapse—not even close.

So why is it that so many have bought into this illusion? Perhaps in part it is because the Lehman Brothers failure was staggering in terms of actual dollars ($639 billion in assets and $619 billion in debt).[11] At first glance, the reader's initial reaction might be that Cahn has surely made his case on at least this point—but he has not.

Even if both the assets and the debt of Lehman Brothers, at $1.25 trillion, are added together, this represents an almost immeasurably tiny fraction of the world economy. To put things in perspective, even when compared to just the American economy, with an estimated value of $188 trillion in assets,[12] it comes out to only about 0.6 percent—exceedingly insignificant when compared to what happened when God judged Israel and imposed a seventy-year Shemitah, which was carried out through the Babylonian captivity.

Furthermore, one of the author's own sources states:

> But when one looks closely at what happened in the weeks after the bank's fall—by any measure the most turbulent and dramatic period in the last 75 years of financial history—*Lehman's collapse was not in fact to blame* for pushing global markets and the economy over the edge.[13]

Where is the precise parallel that Cahn claims? Where is the Shemitah? Once again, it is an illusion.

The stock market crash

Cahn continues to try to build his case by citing the September 29, 2008, stock market crash as the "greatest single-day stock market crash in Wall Street history."[14] He does mention that it was the biggest drop in terms of *points*—but only once. It was not, however, the biggest *percentage* drop by any means. Yet Cahn declares over and over that it was the "biggest crash in Wall Street history":

> [THE PROPHET] "It was the climactic moment of the global implosion and *the greatest single-day stock market crash in Wall*

Street history. Why did it happen?" he asked. "Why did it happen just when it did?"

[KAPLAN] I didn't answer. He paused before revealing the answer.

[THE PROPHET] "*The greatest single-day stock market crash in Wall Street history* took place on the twenty-ninth day of Elul—the critical and crowning day of the Hebrew Shemitah."

[KAPLAN] "My God!" I exclaimed. It was the only thing that could've come out of my mouth at that moment.

[THE PROPHET] "The day when financial accounts must be wiped away," he said.[15]

When God imposed a Shemitah on ancient Israel, everything was wiped away. This is not what happened in 2008. As Cahn points out in the book, the drop in the Dow Jones industrial average was 7 percent.[16] What he does not mention is that this drop does not even rank in the historical top ten in terms of percentages.[17] Not only would Israel have survived such a meager judgment; it could have continued to thrive.

To be fair, the Dow did drop a total of about 25 percent in the two weeks following the defeat of the bailout bill in the U.S. Congress on September 29. Once again, however, this does not rank in the same league as the 1929 market collapse. Not only did it fall 48 percent in just over two months, but by the time the crash had run its course, stocks had lost 90 percent of their value.[18] Yet even that horrendous financial crisis, which triggered the Great Depression, was not nearly of the same relative magnitude as the devastation experienced by ancient Israel. Cahn's treatment of the entire scenario demonstrates just how easily statistics can be manipulated to support almost anything.

Even setting that aside for a moment, given Cahn's reasoning, if the 2008 crash and Great Recession were part of an imposed Shemitah, what about the 1929 crash and the Great Depression? What about the other major market crashes that actually do rank among the top ten worst crashes? Were each of these also a Shemitah judgment?

The overstatements continue to the degree that one would think it would be difficult for even Cahn's most ardent supporters to stand with him:

[THE PROPHET] "The crashing of stock markets across the world meant that the funds invested had vanished and would not be paid back, at least not for the foreseeable future. Both credit and debt, trillions of dollars worth of credit and debt, had, in effect, been canceled. *'Every creditor who has made a loan to his neighbor will let it go, will cancel it'* . . . a Shemitah."

[KAPLAN] "How far back did it go," I asked, "the cancellation of debt in the Shemitah?"

[THE PROPHET] "Back to the end of the last Shemitah," he replied, "to the last remission of debt."

[KAPLAN] "So the Shemitah would *wipe away all the debts of the previous seven years*?"

[THE PROPHET] "Yes."

[KAPLAN] "And when the stock market crashed in September 2008, how much was wiped away?"

[THE PROPHET] "All the gains of the past seven years, and then some."[19]

All credit and debt from 2001 to 2008 had "in effect, been canceled?" There were certainly a lot of losses experienced by both creditors and investors, but nowhere close to all debt was wiped away. Just the simple fact that many people ended up upside down on their mortgages as the housing market collapsed and many lost their homes because of foreclosures clearly demonstrates this. The overstatement here is breathtaking. If debt had been wiped away, these people could have kept their homes and owed nothing.

Another crucial issue that could be easy to miss is the fact that the author has just *redefined the Shemitah itself*. The biblical Shemitah involved the cancellation of all debt owed to creditors. However, Cahn has completely redefined it, with no scriptural support whatsoever, to include *the wiping out of savings and investments*. This is more than misleading. Why is he not being called out on this by every serious student of the Word of God?

And the speculation does not end there. Cahn goes so far as to argue that God was imposing a *global* Shemitah made up of countless smaller ones all over the world:

> [KAPLAN] "And it touched the entire world."

> [THE PROPHET] "It touched the entire global economy in the form of collapsing markets, vanishing investments, government bailouts, corporate and personal bankruptcies, and foreclosures . . . each of which was, in effect, a financial nullification."

> [KAPLAN] "So, in each case, whether by bankruptcy, by aid, or by vanishing accounts, the burden was remitted . . . released . . . each becomes a form of Shemitah."

> [THE PROPHET] "Not only each," he said, "but all . . . the whole. The global economic collapse was, itself, one colossal Shemitah . . . made up of countless smaller ones."[20]

This is so far beyond the realm of reasonable logic, so thoroughly contradicted by historical facts, and so completely devoid of any biblical support, that it simply requires no rebuttal other than to say, "It did not happen." It is a mere illusion—and not a convincing one at that.

The date coincidence

The book traces a series of events in the financial realm in the month of September 2008, which is generally regarded as the beginning of the "Great Recession" and the "Global Economic Crisis." These included the problems with Fannie Mae and Freddie Mac, as well as with Lehman brothers. Then on September 29, the stock market crashed more than 700 points.[21]

As Cahn points out, September 29, 2008, was also the 29th of Elul on the Hebrew calendar. Sunset on Elul 29 marks the end of the year, according to Hebrew reckoning, when all debts among the Jewish people are to be forgiven according to the *mitzvah* (commandment) of Shemitah.

He further notes that precisely seven years earlier on Elul 29 (September 17, 2001, on the Gregorian calendar) the largest stock market crash up to that time had taken place in the wake of 9/11:

> [THE PROPHET] "It happened on Monday, September 17, 2001. It took place in the economic realm, and it would match . . . and

would foreshadow what would happen seven years later."

[KAPLAN] "And it was . . . "

[THE PROPHET] "It was the greatest stock market point crash in Wall Street history up to that day. The record would remain intact for seven years, seven years until the crash of 2008. Take note, Nouriel, of what we have."

[KAPLAN] "What do we have?" I asked.

[THE PROPHET] "A seven-year period that begins with a stock market crash and ends with a second stock market crash. We have a seven-year period framed by the two greatest stock market crashes in Wall Street history up to that time."

[KAPLAN] "A seven-year cycle beginning and concluding with two massive remissions of credit and debt."

[THE PROPHET] "Which is what?"

[KAPLAN] "The Shemitah," I answered.[22]

As has already been noted, the reader has been somewhat misled because *these crashes did not rank in even the top ten largest crashes in terms of percentages.*

Admittedly the timing is interesting, but is it significant? If any of the other proposed harbingers in the book genuinely pointed to divine origin, it might be easier to take this detail more seriously. The fact that Cahn has given an unbiblical definition to Shemitah doesn't help. Nor does the fact that the Shemitah was never required of any nation except Israel. Then there is the problem that the stock market crashes of 2001 and 2008 came nowhere close to the Shemitah that God imposed on Israel.

"Trying to have it both ways" is a recurring issue in the methods Cahn uses as he tries to collect and correlate evidence for his theories. He does this again concerning the seven years between 2001 and 2008—so much so that it has the feel of his being far too selective in choosing which facts to present and which to leave out. Of course, every author has to be selective, but in this case the result is to make it very difficult for readers to objectively evaluate the entire body of evidence for themselves. Readers are not necessarily being misinformed, but they are being left uninformed.

In order to make his case for the exact seven-year "Shemitah timing" between the stock market crashes, he appeals to the *Hebrew calendar* to show that both happened on the last day of the Jewish year, Elul 29. That seems reasonable. However, he shifts to the *Gregorian calendar* (the one normally used) to show the precision of the seven years between 9/11/2001 and 9/11/2008:

> [THE PROPHET] "The collapse of Lehman Brothers and the American economy took place over the course of one week. It was the anniversary week of another American calamity . . ."

> [KAPLAN] "9/11."

> [THE PROPHET] "Yes, 9/11," he said. "The collapse of Fannie Mae and Freddie Mac happened on September 7. The collapse of Lehman Brothers began two days later on September 9 when it lost 45 percent of its value. It was on September 10 that it announced its loss of almost four billion dollars. The following day its stock took a second precipitous plunge."

> [KAPLAN] "September 11."[23]

Here Cahn uses the Gregorian calendar (which is used in America) when it suits his purposes to show precise timing. Then to show the precise timing of another set of events, he uses the Hebrew calendar to demonstrate that the two collapses of the stock market on 29 Elul matched the seven-year cycle of the Shemitah. So economic cycles follow the Hebrew calendar? Not necessarily, as can be seen when Cahn tries to muster additional support for his theory:

> [KAPLAN] "And the time separating the two events . . . "

> [THE PROPHET] "Seven years," said The Prophet. "There were seven years between the two."

> [KAPLAN] "Seven years—the biblical period of time that concerns a nation's financial and economic realms."[24]

In this case, he isn't talking about seven years based on the Hebrew calendar. He's talking about September 11, 2001, and September 11, 2008—according to the Gregorian calendar.

Beyond this, the way that he deals with the dates is also rather questionable. Things happened on various dates *around* September 11, 2008, but he picks out that date to argue for the precision:

> [THE PROPHET] "So not only did the collapse of 2008 take place at the seven-year mark from 9/11, but it specifically concerned the principle of the Shemitah.

Fannie Mae and Freddie Mac collapsed on September 7. Lehman Brothers' stock dropped 45 percent on September 9 and then announced a $4 billion dollar loss on September 10. And then on September 11, Lehman's stock "took a second precipitous plunge." But why is September 11 considered *the* significant date and not September 15, which is the day it filed for bankruptcy? Or why not September 9, when the drop started? This seems very arbitrary and gives the impression of "cherry-picking" evidence in order to strengthen the author's arguments while diminishing the significance of related evidence that does not support and, in many ways, even undercuts his arguments.

Some might suggest that such criticisms miss the larger important point while unnecessarily getting lost in minute details. However, if Cahn relies on this level of precise detail, then his claims need to be examined at that level. When this is done, the claimed precision required by the Shemitah begins to fade away.

Once again, the author cannot have it both ways by arguing for exact precision to the day, on one hand, but then arguing for "in-the-ballpark" precision on the other—especially by switching between two different ways of reckoning dates (the Hebrew and Gregorian calendars). This is not significantly different from using the Septuagint to prove one point and the Masoretic text to prove another point—even though they are mutually contradictory.

The "mystery of sevens"

Someone has well said, "If you torture statistics long enough, they will confess to anything."

A significant feature of Cahn's ongoing argument is what he calls "a mystery of sevens,"[25] which relies on numbers and statistics. This refers to several occurrences of the number seven such that together coincidence is not a reasonable explanation, meaning that the pattern must be a sign from God. Cahn cites three instances where seven appears in association with the Shemitah and thus "demonstrates divine intervention":

1. $700 billion: The amount of Lehman Brothers' rejected government bailout request

2. 7%: The size of the stock market crash by percentage in 2008 on the day that Congress voted down the bailout

3. 777: The size of that stock market crash by points

Could the Lord do this? Yes, He certainly could. Does He still do this? Yes, He very well may. And if He has, then anyone would be insanely foolish to ignore His warning.

Of course, the number seven undoubtedly has special significance throughout the Bible. Among the many things tied to the number seven are the number of days in a week, the Sabbath day, the number of generations between Adam and Enoch, the number of animals required for the burnt offering, the month of the Feasts of Trumpets and Tabernacles, the Day of Atonement, and of course the Shemitah (Sabbath year). In the book of Revelation, seven is the number of the churches in Asia Minor, the number of the Spirits of God, the number of judgments in each of the three series among others.

So, the significance of the number seven is clearly biblical. That is not the issue. The issue is whether Cahn has correctly identified the hand of God through these occurrences of the number seven. Unfortunately, Cahn's insistence on making significant claims based on precise statistics forces a fairly tedious analysis of the details. However, as the analysis will show, by arguing for such detailed precision, he ends up falling on his own sword.

Failed Lehman Brothers bailout

As one would expect, this failed bailout involves a huge number of statistics. However, an examination of the evidence shows that the number seven actually appears in very few places and simply does not support the claim. The following are just a few of the many related statistics:[26]

1. $2.8 billion: 2008 second fiscal quarter losses

2. $6 billion: Amount of assets sold because of the above losses

3. 73%: Loss of value in first half of 2008

4. 6%: Amount of assets sold because of the above losses

5. 9/15/2008: Date of bankruptcy filing

6. $639 billion: Assets

7. $619 billion: Debt

8. $10 billion: Erosion of market capitalization in 2008

9. $86.18: The record the stock price hit in 2007

10. 3/13/2007: Largest one-day stock drop in five years

11. 2500: Number of mortgage-related jobs eliminated in August 2007

12. 77%: Stock drop in first week of September 2008

13. 93%: Stock plunge on September 15, 2008

The above list is fully representative of all the statistics and is not intentionally selective. Cahn has chosen to focus on only one number—700 (he does not cite the 77 percent drop in the first week of September). Can that single number really be counted as an amazing match for which only God could be responsible? Does 700 even count as a seven? Perhaps 777, but 700?

How does Cahn justify picking just one number from such a large universe of statistics in order to prove his point? Using this method, the author could have been trying to prove any number from zero through nine and found the evidence he was looking for. The suggestion that the number 700 has any significance is just not reasonable.

And finally, an interesting fact is that although Congress allowed Lehman Brothers to fail by voting down their $700 billion bailout on Monday, September 29, on Friday of that week the bailout was approved for the financial sector in general.[27] Once again, the reader has been misled through the very selective use of facts that do not remotely represent the whole picture—and the total proof is now down from three points to two.

Stock market crash of 2008

As he does on several occasions, in trying to demonstrate the validity of the "mystery of sevens," Cahn appeals to what he says are very precise numbers. Therefore, if precision is claimed to prove God's involvement, the numbers actually need to be precise. Anything less proves nothing more than an interesting coincidence.

The first issue is the supposed sign of the 777-point drop on September 29, 2008. Late that day, CNNMoney.com reported the drop as 778 points.[28] This was because the actual figure was 777.68 points. It was not 777, nor could it properly be rounded down to 777.

If the Lord were trying to draw attention to what He was doing, causing the drop to be precisely 777.77 or 777.00 certainly would be no more difficult for Him than 777.68. But as it is, the actual figure is just another number.

Of course, the charge could be made that this is just wrangling over insignificant details and missing the main point. However, it is the *details* on which Cahn's theories depend, and in this case, the theory is dashed on the rocks of those details. This takes the total proof down to just one final point.

As has been previously noted, the corresponding 7 percent drop does not even rank in the top 10 declines by percentage points. Furthermore, while the DOW is an important measure, the NASDAQ and S&P 500 indexes are also significant indicators, and they fell 9.1 percent and 8.8 percent respectively.[29] How does the author determine which one of the three important stock market numbers is a sign from God? Would it have also been a sign if the DOW had fallen 8 percent but the NASDAQ had fallen 7 percent?

And finally, the fact is that the drop was not exactly 7.0 percent. Rather, it was 6.98 percent.[30] Citing this exact number will surely cause some to roll their eyes at the meager two-hundredths difference. However, when the basis for one's arguments is precise numbers, then they need to be precise. Would it also have been a sign if it had been 6.51percent or 7.49 percent? How much could it be off and still be a sign?

This is not 722 B.C., when numbers were considered precise if they were in the ballpark. In the twenty-first century, with incredibly precise computers and lightning-fast communications technology, millions of dollars are often at stake with even just 1 hundredth of a percent. For example, 2 hundredths of 1 percent of the $700 billion bailout is $14 million. If God were sending a sign, how difficult would it have been for Him to make it exactly a 7.0 percent drop? Or better still, 7.7 percent, or even 7.77 percent?

This is not to presume to tell the Lord how He should send signs or with what precision. On the other hand, if someone claims to try to discern what God has done with precision, then precision should be expected. Yet the degree of precision that Cahn employs is both arbitrary and inconsistent. The numbers are interesting—but not amazing. They do not rise to the level of being the sure signature of the hand of God.

This is compounded by the fact that it is impossible to justify the very narrow selectivity that Cahn uses. This is "stacking the deck." The mathematical improbability argument to which so many appeal in support of the validity of the author's theories simply evaporates under even moderate scrutiny. This removes all three numbers from the "mystery of the sevens," leaving just the dates themselves to consider.

The most obvious problem is that if the three numbers have no statistical significance, then the significance of the date on which they occurred is lessened dramatically. Granted, the timing of what happened on these two dates is perhaps the most interesting phenomenon in the book, but this is simply because none of the rest of the "evidence" has any demonstrable significance.

Cahn has noted that the "first shaking" occurred on September 17, 2001 (29 Elul), in the form of a stock market crash on the last day of the Shemitah year. For that to be significant would require the *previous seven years* to also be part of an imposed Shemitah cycle, beginning with September 6, 1994 (1 Tishri).

Another consideration is that in 2001 the drop was 684 points at 7.1 percent.[31] Close, perhaps, but this is even less precise than in 2008. Can it be said with any confidence that God caused this drop as a warning to America? And did He do so in a way that would be recognized as connected to the

Jewish Shemitah? To even suggest that this might be true requires a lot of supporting evidence, which simply doesn't exist.

No one else has noticed this over the last eleven years for a very good reason—it is not obvious. And if it isn't obvious, then it isn't a sign or warning of judgment. Cahn says that there was a second warning in 2008 because everyone ignored the first warning in 2001. No, they didn't. It was not ignored—it wasn't seen.

Of all the godly men and women across America who love and serve the Lord, of the thousands and thousands of outstanding Bible teachers and preachers, virtually no one was sounding the alarm because they did not recognize it as a warning of an impending Shemitah judgment. The reason they did not recognize it is because *the evidence is not there and the idea of a Shemitah being imposed on America is unbiblical.*

THE SHEMITAH AS LAW

The myriad of practical problems strongly mitigates against Cahn's theory that God has imposed a Shemitah on the United States. As previously noted, Cahn acknowledges that the Shemitah was given to Israel and not to any other nation. But the theological problem involved with proposing that God is still using the Shemitah as a principle is even greater.

The Sabbath day and the Sabbath year, the Shemitah, were exclusively part of the Law of Moses. If God had any expectations of man with regard to the Sabbath day or a seven-year economic or agricultural cycle apart from the Law, there would be corresponding revelation. However, the Scriptures are silent on this, both before and after the Law.

The New Testament neither prescribes nor describes any Sabbath-keeping for believers after Christ's death on the cross. There are only seven references to the Sabbath day after the Day of Pentecost (Acts 2). These references occur only in the book of Acts in chapters 13 through 18 and are only in reference to the day of the week when unconverted Jews gathered in the synagogues.

Other than these, there are no references to the Sabbath day or year—not a single instruction to the churches—except for one important passage in Romans concerning Sabbath-keeping:

Romans 14:5-6—

> One person esteems one day above another; another esteems every day alike. Let each be fully convinced in his own mind. He who observes the day, observes it to the Lord; and he who does not observe the day, to the Lord he does not observe it. He who eats, eats to the Lord, for he gives God thanks; and he who does not eat, to the Lord he does not eat, and gives God thanks.

In keeping with this principle, the writer of Hebrews gives additional insight into the theological basis for what Paul wrote to the believers in Rome. In order to prepare ethnically Jewish Christians for the soon-coming destruction of the temple, chapter 4 makes it clear that those who have believed the gospel have entered into God's Sabbath rest—which would include both the Sabbath day and the Sabbath year:

Hebrews 4:1-3, 8-10—

> Therefore, since a promise remains of entering His rest, let us fear lest any of you seem to have come short of it. For indeed the gospel was preached to us as well as to them; but the word which they heard did not profit them, not being mixed with faith in those who heard it. For we who have believed do enter that rest . . .

> For if Joshua had given them rest, then He would not afterward have spoken of another day. There remains therefore a rest for the people of God. For he who has entered His rest has himself also ceased from his works as God did from His.

Those who are in Christ by faith have entered into the Sabbath rest that God has promised and prepared. Apart from Christ there is no Sabbath requirement, meaning that because Christ fulfilled the Law, God does not impose a Sabbath day or a Sabbath year (the Shemitah).

God no longer expects Jews to continue keeping the Sabbath day or Shemitah. Rather, His desire is that they would enter His Sabbath through faith in Christ. Gentiles were *never* required to keep either Sabbath. Therefore, there is no biblical basis whatsoever for Cahn's theory concerning an imposed Shemitah. Quite the opposite is true—his theory runs counter to the Word of God and the gospel.

THE SHEMITAH: CONCLUDING THOUGHTS

Together, this all explains why no one else has seen this for so many years—except for Cahn, who has a propensity for seeking hidden mysteries in obscure passages (as will be seen later in this book). The Bible teachers and theologians who have endorsed *The Harbinger* need to ask themselves why they did not see this imposed Shemitah. If it is now so obvious, how could they have missed it? There is no new information, no new revelation from God. The only thing new is profound speculation.

Beyond this, if God were sending a specific warning through a specific set of circumstances in order to bring America to repentance, why would He make the signs so obscure and imprecise as to be virtually impossible to recognize? And if this is all part of a parallel or pattern, why are there no biblical examples of God being so cryptic in warning of impending judgment? God's warnings were almost universally clear and could not be missed. They were ignored, but they were not missed or misunderstood.

And finally, the imposed-Shemitah theory is thoroughly unbiblical at its core. It is antithetical to the biblical concept of the Sabbath laws given to Israel alone and the fulfillment of those laws for believers in Christ.

This doesn't mean that God will not judge the nations, including America. This doesn't mean that His judgment is not already underway. It may very well be—and if so, it is well deserved. However, whatever the judgment is or will be, it is not an imposed Shemitah judgment connected with Isaiah 9:10.

CHAPTER 15

A KING AND A PRESIDENT

CONFIRMATION OF THE ISRAEL–AMERICA LINK

AS PREVIOUSLY NOTED, Nouriel Kaplan, the journalist, has a dream about the dedication of the temple in Jerusalem under King Solomon. Although the author has said that this dream is simply part of the fictional storyline, the idea of connecting Solomon and George Washington is clearly far more than just a surprising plot-twist.

Furthermore, Cahn goes well beyond just connecting them in some vague sort of way—King Solomon actually transforms *into* George Washington on the Temple Mount. Cahn could hardly state more directly that he believes this goes far beyond just some superficial parallelism between the establishment of ancient Israel and the establishment of the United States as an independent nation.

Although preceded by kings Saul and David, it was Solomon who built and dedicated the temple. This finalized the establishment of Israel as a nation because it was at that time that God came to dwell among His people once again—not in a temporary tent but in a permanent structure. So, too, the inauguration of George Washington finalized the establishment of the United States as a nation. The factual message that Cahn believes he is communicating through this fictional literary device is unmistakable, though not surprising, by this point in the book.

How can Cahn continue to deny that he has connected ancient Israel and America together in *The Harbinger* when Kaplan explicitly states that they are linked?

> [KAPLAN] "Solomon was the king of Israel. Washington was the first president of the United States. There was something in the *linking of ancient Israel and America, as with all the other mysteries.*"[1]

CONSECRATION AS COVENANT NATIONS

Despite repeated denials to the contrary, Cahn seems to affirm once again that America is in a covenant relationship with God. As part of his explanation of the dream, The Prophet says, "The nation's ground of consecration will become its ground of judgment."[2] A few pages later, Kaplan has traced the consecration of the United States to God's purposes to the first capital, New York City—and more specifically to St. Paul's Chapel, "The place where America was dedicated to God"[3]—which is located at Ground Zero.

In other words, a harbinger has appeared in America just as it had in Israel. The place of Israel's consecration, the temple, was destroyed, while the place of America's consecration was also destroyed. Then Cahn directly connects the place of destruction to Israel's covenant with God:

> [THE PROPHET] "The Temple Mount represented the nation's covenant with God. So its destruction was the ultimate sign that the covenant was broken."[4]

Just prior to this statement, as he has before, Cahn introduces yet another extrabiblical idea into the story as if it were an inviolable principle, which it is not. While interacting with Kaplan to help him understand the dream with Solomon and Washington, The Prophet makes the following statement:

> "This, Nouriel, is a critical principle. Take note of it. When judgment comes to such a nation once committed to God and once consecrated to His purposes, but now departed from His ways, the judgment will return to its ground of consecration, or to put it more concisely: 'The nation's ground of consecration will become the ground of its judgment.'"

Where did Cahn find this principle? Not in the Bible. Yes, Israel's place of consecration, the temple, was destroyed. However, unless the Bible presents a general principle by making a statement that reflects a "timeless truth" (like the many in Proverbs) or something happens enough times to establish a pattern, saying that a one-time event like this establishes a principle is nothing more than conjecture.

However, if one does try to apply this principle as introduced by Cahn, then what the logic and the supposed parallel demands is inescapable: The destruction of the place of consecration in both nations was a sign that each nation's covenant with God had been broken—both Israel's covenant and America's covenant. By insisting on pressing every detail as he has, Cahn has either tipped his hand as to what he really believes, or he has made a serious mistake that needs to be corrected. No one could come to any other conclusion but that he is saying that Israel and the United States are both God's chosen covenant nations.

Even in the midst of this problem there is yet another fact that many people have apparently overlooked—a not-so-minor detail that concerns the actual destruction of "the holy place of consecration," the temple in Jerusalem. This was a climactic event in the dream, which set the stage for The Prophet to announce the above-mentioned principle. In complete contradiction to Cahn's theory, however, the holy place of consecration in New York City, St. Paul's Chapel, was barely touched by the destruction of 9/11, being shielded by the sycamore of Ground Zero. Given the emphasis Cahn places on the destruction of the temple, the problem of St. Paul's Chapel is insurmountable. The supposed parallel and pattern simply did not happen at all.

Incidentally, the place of Washington's inauguration, Federal Hall, was razed in 1812 and replaced with the present building (now a national memorial), which is built after the pattern of a Greek temple.[5] Although this building suffered some structural damage on 9/11, it did not fall either and is still in use. Therefore, this does not help to support the claim that a parallel is in effect either.

One additional problem (though overlooked by most) concerns the actual ceremony of America's consecration as a "Christian nation." Cahn's entire argument is built on the idea that America was once a Christian nation, dedicated to God's purposes and that George Washington led the way as did Solomon in ancient Israel.

A lot of debate surrounds the question of whether Washington was actually a born-again believer, with a fair amount of evidence on both sides. That question goes far beyond the scope of this book. But what is *not* debatable is the historical fact that George Washington was deeply involved in Freemasonry—and this was clearly evident during the consecration ceremony.

The George Washington Masonic Memorial building is located in Alexandria, Virginia. The official website describes the significance of the memorial:

> The George Washington Masonic Memorial is more than a colossal memorial and museum. It is a tourist attraction and destination; research center and library; community center; performing arts center and concert hall; banquet and celebration site; and meeting site for local and countless visiting Masonic lodges and organizations. However, first and foremost, it is a memorial to honor and perpetuate the memory, character and virtues of the man who best exemplifies what Freemasons are and ought to be, Brother George Washington.[6]

By the time that Washington became President of the United States, he had been a Freemason for thirty-seven years—however, not just any Freemason:

> The Lodge at Alexandria, Virginia was first warranted by the Provincial Grand Lodge of Pennsylvania on February 3, 1783, as Lodge No. 39. . . .On April 22, 1788, the Lodge received a Charter from the Grand Lodge of Virginia as Alexandria Lodge No. 22. The Lodge asked Washington to be its Charter Master under the Virginia Charter and he agreed. Washington was inaugurated as the First President of the United States on April 30, 1789 while holding the office of Master of Alexandria Lodge. After his death on December 14, 1799, the Lodge was renamed Alexandria-Washington Lodge No. 22, by the Grand Lodge of Virginia.[7]

Additional information on this website demonstrates that Washington's Freemasonry was not merely a formal and incidental part of his life but was rather a foundational principle:

During the War for Independence, General Washington attended Masonic celebration and religious observances in several states. He also supported Masonic Lodges that formed within army regiments.

At his first inauguration in 1791 [actually 1789, as noted later on the same web page], President Washington took his oath of office on a Bible from St. John's Lodge in New York. During his two terms, he visited Masons in North and South Carolina and presided over the cornerstone ceremony for the U.S. Capitol in 1793.

In retirement, Washington became charter Master of the newly chartered Alexandria Lodge No. 22, sat for a portrait in his Masonic regalia, and in death, was buried with Masonic honors.

Such was Washington's character, that from almost the day he took his Masonic obligations until his death, he became the same man in private that he was in public. In Masonic terms, he remained "a just and upright Mason" and became a true Master Mason. Washington was, in Masonic terms, a "living stone" who became the cornerstone of American civilization.

If someone objects that this has nothing to do with the inauguration ceremony itself, MasonicWorld.com notes:

> He was the first, and to date only Mason serving as Master of a Lodge when inaugurated. Also of interest was the Masonic atmosphere at his inaugural ceremony —the presence of Brother Masons and the Great Light of Freemasonry, The Holy Bible, provided by a Masonic Lodge, St. Johns No. 1 of New York.[8]

"Right Worshipful Master" Captain Kenneth Force has noted that the procession from Federal Hall to St. Paul's Chapel continues to be reenacted by Masons in New York:

> After the balcony ceremony, President Washington entered the Senate chamber and delivered his inauguration address to the assembled Congress. Then, in another procession, he left Federal Hall and proceeded with the Vice President to nearby St. Paul's Chapel of Trinity Church for religious services. (A practice followed to this day by New York Masons, who have reenacted the oath-taking ceremony for many years.)

As previously noted, in 1793, Washington, as Acting Grand Master, laid the cornerstone for the U.S. Capitol building.[9] In 1794, Washington sat for a portrait in "Masonic regalia at the request of Alexandria Lodge." Then, on December 18, 1799, Washington was "buried at Mount Vernon with Masonic rites as well as those of the church, conducted by Alexandria Lodge."[10]

The question that must be asked is, What god was being invoked in the Masonic-dominated inauguration and consecration? The deeply embedded Masonic involvement in the inauguration of Washington and the consecration of the United States does serious damage to Cahn's theories. However, in his public response to T. A. McMahon's review of *The Harbinger*, Cahn openly ridiculed this author because of concerns with the "historical facts" of America's beginnings:

> *The Harbinger* states that those who founded America *viewed* it as a new Israel and in covenant with God. The statement was simply a basic historical statement known by most students of American History 101. Yet the man who claimed this was apparently unable to discern the difference between an historical fact and a theological proposition. He even labeled, on the air, this very statement as "dangerous." So the fruit of all this "discernment" is that we've now come to the point of publicly denouncing basic historical statements as "dangerous."[11]

That Cahn chose this particular tack as a line of defense seems somewhat disingenuous given the many historical facts concerning the Masonic nature of certain aspects of America's birth as a nation, which Cahn apparently overlooked—and has since dismissed as irrelevant.

WHICH COVENANT? ABRAHAMIC OR MOSAIC?

Cahn refers only to Israel's destruction but never to its restoration as modern-day Israel. Neither does he ever mention that national Israel still has a place in God's program in the future—that Jerusalem will be the capital of the messianic kingdom. With these two significant omissions, Cahn leaves the reader with the unmistakable impression that Israel is finished as a nation (which many Christians already believe) and that he is suggesting that America very well may constitute a new Israel.

The issue of a relationship between Israel's destruction and a broken covenant raises a supremely important question that Cahn does not answer. Exactly which covenant did Israel break? Was it the Mosaic covenant or the Abrahamic covenant? This is not merely an academic question.

The foundation of America has been in view throughout the book, but it was upon the foundation of the Abrahamic covenant that the nation of Israel was established. If Cahn is somehow proposing that Israel managed to break the Abrahamic covenant, then that means that God is finished with national Israel. However, the Bible makes it very clear that *the Abrahamic covenant is a unilateral, unconditional, and eternal covenant, whose ultimate fulfillment depends solely on the faithfulness of God.* If that covenant can be broken, then God cannot be trusted.

This means that Israel could have broken only the bilateral, conditional Mosaic covenant—which is exactly what the Scriptures teach. But that immediately raises the question concerning America and which type of covenant Cahn thinks was broken that led to the destruction of America's place of dedication.

Biblical covenants represent one of the most important and foundational theological concepts in the Word of God. They must be handled carefully and precisely. By failing to do so, Cahn has introduced theological ambiguity and confusion concerning the future of both Israel and the United States, which needs to be cleared up somehow.

SOLOMON'S PROPHETIC WORD TO AMERICA

In chapter 20, Cahn once again demonstrates that there is a discrepancy between what he now says he meant in the book and what he actually wrote. Although he emphatically denies believing that Isaiah's prophecy is to America, he confirms his belief that Old Testament prophecies can be directly applied to America in the following exchange concerning a prophetic word from Solomon to America:

> [KAPLAN] "No. I woke up. But it was Washington's message, the warning for a nation that disregards the eternal rules of heaven."

[THE PROPHET] "Yes," he replied, "that's part of the message. But in your dream, it wasn't just Washington. Washington and King Solomon were joined together."

[THE PROPHET] "So the message is twofold. There's another part to it, another prophetic word, and this time from King Solomon."

[KAPLAN] "From King Solomon to America?"

[THE PROPHET] "For that nation that has turned from God, for that nation from which the smiles of heaven have been withdrawn."

[KAPLAN] "And this word came during the dedication of the Temple?" I asked.

[THE PROPHET] "It came when the dedication was finished."[12]

Cahn has once again used a question to make what surely seems to be a statement. He has Kaplan following The Prophet's explanation of the dream sequence and anticipating the obvious conclusion: "From King Solomon to America?" The Prophet responds to Kaplan's question about King Solomon by using Washington's words. This response is just ambiguous enough that Cahn can sidestep the charge of stating that Solomon's words also contained a prophecy to both America and Israel.

Though he might avoid this charge on a technicality, anyone would understand that he is only confirming and reinforcing what he has repeatedly affirmed elsewhere concerning Isaiah's prophecy. Cahn then reveals that the "prophetic word" from Solomon to Israel was 2 Chronicles 7:14, which can now be applied to America:

[KAPLAN] The Prophet then handed me a Bible, a little black Bible, small enough to fit into someone's shirt pocket.

[THE PROPHET] "Open it up," he said, "to the Book of 2 Chronicles, chapter 7, verse 14. And read it."

[KAPLAN] So I opened it and read the words out loud:

"If My people who are called by My name will humble themselves, and pray and seek My face, and turn from their wicked ways, then I will hear from heaven, and will forgive their sin and heal their land."

[THE PROPHET] "That's the word, Nouriel. That's the word appointed for America."

[KAPLAN] "If My people," I said. "And who are `My people'?"

[THE PROPHET] "As given to Solomon, My people would refer to the nation as a whole, and, more specifically, those within the nation who could genuinely be called the people of God, those who followed His ways."

[KAPLAN] "And what would it mean applied now to America?"

[THE PROPHET] "It's the call of God to a nation once dedicated to His purposes but now falling away from His will. It's the call of God to return."

Second Chronicles 7:14 is probably one of the most frequently misused quotes in the Old Testament. The verse is often quoted apart from the literary context. In other cases, it is quoted in the context of the theology that says that America is also a "chosen nation." It is frequently found in an American patriotic context and is viewed as a principle and a promise and a call for the nation to return to her historic Christian roots. As important as it is for the people of any nation to be in fellowship with God, a closer study of the passage reveals that this is an inappropriate application of the words God said to King Solomon.

Cahn's use of 2 Chronicles 7:14 is consistent with the popular view, but it involves extrapolating the phrase "My people" beyond what the biblical text allows. The phrase "My people" occurs in a total of 220 verses—in 214 Old Testament verses and in 6 New Testament verses. In every verse, except for Revelation 18:4 where it refers to Tribulation saints, "My people" always refers to the nation of Israel.

The mistake that many make when handling this passage is to interpret the verse as embodying a spiritual principle that is broadly applicable to any nation in general—and to the United States specifically. The thinking is that "My people" can also be applied to America because her founders frequently invoked God and because the nation has long been considered a Christian nation.

As always, however, the context governs the specific meaning of any word or phrase and, in context, this is not meant to be a general principle. "My people" not only refers to Israel initially but to Israel *exclusively* as part of a promise given in light of the Abrahamic and Davidic covenants. No other nation can lay claim to the title "My people" in even a generic sense because it is a precise theological designation.

Of course, all believers are in the category of "God's people," but that is in a different sense. In 2 Chronicles, "My people" refers to God's chosen *nation* of Israel—which ideally would be made up entirely of believers, but unfortunately that has not been the case historically.

Furthermore, the promise connected with repentance not only has a spiritual component: *the Lord will forgive their sins*; but it also has a physical component: *He will also heal their land*. God's judgment of sin manifests itself through physical harm, whether through the forces of nature or the forces of a foreign invader, both of which bring destruction. The promise to Israel is that God will be involved personally in the physical restoration from judgment.

The church does not constitute an earthly nation, nor does it have any physical land—so the promise of 2 Chronicles 7:14 cannot be applied to America nor even to just the believers in America. Any attempt to make just a *spiritual* application is to either ignore half of the promise or to allegorize the passage by making the church the spiritual equivalent of national Israel. This would once again introduce the problem of replacement theology.

Although Cahn is in good company in the way he connects 2 Chronicles 7:14 to America, this is not the way that either Solomon or the Lord intended for this promise to be understood. There is no way to properly apply the passage as a general principle to any nation or to any group of people except national Israel. This being the case, it is even more inappropriate to tie this king and this president together as Cahn has.

CHAPTER 16

PREPARING FOR ETERNITY

THE UNITED STATES has deeply rooted spiritual problems that are destroying the very foundations of this country. Murder, violence, immorality, crime, corruption, substance abuse, destruction of the family, hatred, greed—the list is virtually endless. But is it significantly different from the days of Noah, when the wickedness of man was so great that "every intent of the thoughts of his heart was only evil continually"?[1]

In light of this, Jonathan Cahn has written a book with a hard-hitting message that focuses directly on the need for America to repent or face the possibility of God's judgment. Without question, he is to be commended for his desire to proclaim that the country needs to turn to the Lord. He chose the fictional format to reach as many as possible with this message, and he has achieved impressive results with an audience of a size that relatively few books ever achieve. This is significant.

He also rightly notes that national repentance can take place only at a personal level—when people individually turn to God. Because of this, chapter 21, "Eternity," is perhaps the most important one in the book.

Cahn does an excellent job of dealing with the matters of sin and judgment. One of the best and most biblical discussions in the entire book is in that section of chapter 21:

> [The Prophet] "Judgment isn't ultimately about nations—but people. As it's written: *'It's appointed for man once to die and then*

judgment.' After the end comes the Day of Judgment, in light of which all other judgment [*sic*] are only foreshadows. And no one is exempt. Each must stand before Him."

[KAPLAN] "Why?"

[THE PROPHET] "Why judgment?"

[KAPLAN] "Yes."

[THE PROPHET] "It must be. As long as there's evil, there has to be judgment. Every sin, every wrong, every evil has to be brought to an end. Without it, there would be no hope."

[KAPLAN] "Without judgment there would be no hope?" I asked.

[THE PROPHET] "Without judgment, there would be no end to evil in the universe . . . or in man's heart. There would be no heaven."[2]

This particular dialogue is quite lengthy, going on for several pages—but the length is justified and the section is quite good. Cahn develops a strong narrative with some helpful illustrations and powerful questions and answers between The Prophet and Kaplan:

[THE PROPHET] "So what we see as the slightest of sins within ourselves appears, in the eyes of Him who is absolute goodness, even more abhorrently evil than the crimes of the Nazis appear to us. In the light of the absolute Good, our lust becomes as adultery and our hatred as murder."

[KAPLAN] "But then who could stand?" I asked. "Who could make it into heaven?"

[THE PROPHET] "No one could stand, and no one could make it into heaven. How far would just one sin take you away from the infinite righteousness of God?"

[KAPLAN] "An infinite distance?"

[THE PROPHET] "Yes. So how far are we from heaven?"

[KAPLAN] "An infinite distance."

[THE PROPHET] "And how great is the judgment?"

[KAPLAN] "Infinitely great."

[THE PROPHET] "And how long would it take us to bridge the gap, to be reconciled to God, to enter heaven?"

[KAPLAN] "An infinity of time."

[THE PROPHET] "Eternity," he said.

[KAPLAN] "So we could never get there, could we?"

[THE PROPHET] "And to be infinitely separated from God and heaven . . . is what?" he asked.

[KAPLAN] "Hell?"

[THE PROPHET] "Hell—infinite separation from God and from all things good; total, infinite, eternal judgment."[3]

The challenge to be spiritually prepared for the day of judgment is unmistakably clear. The eternal consequences of sin before the infinitely holy and righteous God are spelled out in detail. As The Prophet states, "And no one is exempt. Each must stand before Him."[4]

WEAK SCRIPTURAL SUPPORT

It's hard to fault Cahn for very much up to this point in chapter 21 as he discusses sin and judgment. However, one particular weakness that does stand out is the relatively little use of Scripture, either directly or indirectly.

Of the many hundreds of verses in the Bible concerning sin, Cahn refers to only one, Proverbs 16:2—and even that verse only obliquely alludes to man's sinfulness. Likewise, of the hundreds of verses that deal with judgment, he refers only to Isaiah 10:3 ("the day of judgment") and Hebrews 9:27 (the main point of which is not judgment).

Unfortunately, this is a problem thoughout chapter 21, where scripture quotes are critically needed. In the remainder of the chapter, there are only two other direct biblical references: "God is love" (from 1 John 4:8) and "You cannot see the kingdom of God unless you are born again" (from John 3:3).

This is not to say that Cahn doesn't present biblical truth, and he does say many true things. However, only the quoted Word of God can provide the necessary authority to speak of such weighty spiritual matters. The readers of *The Harbinger* need to understand that the author's words about sin and judgment are not merely his own opinions but come directly from the Scriptures. As the Apostle Paul reminds the church at Rome, specifically in the context of proclaiming the gospel, "So then faith comes by hearing, and hearing by the Word of God" (Romans 10:17).

Why The Prophet would quote so few biblical passages is difficult to fathom, particularly in a chapter about salvation. This does not fit the pattern of the biblical prophets. The prophets, including the apostles, did not speak on their own authority. Instead, they most frequently conveyed exactly what they had received from God directly, or they quoted scriptures that were already recognized as the Word of God. As one would expect, the preaching recorded in the Book of Acts includes extensive quotes from Scripture, as do all of the New Testament letters. These men of God understood that making scripturally correct statements is not the same as quoting the Word of God, even when saying the same things. That The Prophet quotes very little from the the Bible is a significant shortcoming of this chapter.

Lest someone object that *The Harbinger* is just fiction, it must be remembered that the parables told by Jesus were entirely fictional—yet they frequently included quotes from the Hebrew Scriptures. The importance of quoting the Word of God cannot be overstated. As the writer of Hebrews put it:

Hebrews 4:12—

> For the word of God is living and powerful, and sharper than any two-edged sword, piercing even to the division of soul and spirit, and of joints and marrow, and is a discerner of the thoughts and intents of the heart.

And as the Apostle Paul reminds Timothy:

2 Timothy 3:16–17—

> All Scripture is given by inspiration of God, and is profitable for doctrine, for reproof, for correction, for instruction in righteousness, that the man of God may be complete, thoroughly equipped for every good work.

Once again, every Bible teacher and every Bible student must always keep in mind that the only authority that anyone has is the authority of the Word of God. The readers of *The Harbinger* need to understand that they are not just being confronted with someone's personal opinions.

A MISSED OPPORTUNITY

Setting aside the overwhelming problems, it could be said that Cahn has "preached" a very powerful "sermon" in the first twenty chapters of the book. Then, as any good evangelist would, he gives an invitation to respond to the message. Cahn's heart and passion for warning people of God's judgment and encouraging repentance are clear throughout the book and particularly in this chapter.

Unfortunately, in addition to the problem of only a few quotes from Scripture, this chapter raises a number of issues directly related to the presentation of the gospel itself. With such an incredibly large audience, a great opportunity has been missed.

A believer, or even an unbeliever who already understands the gospel very well, would probably grasp much of what Cahn is saying about salvation in chapter 21. However, several significant, even crucial, elements of the gospel are either not stated or are not stated clearly enough for the gospel to be understood. Because of this, for someone with no Christian background or with only a vague familiarity with biblical Christianity—perhaps even church-goers in many of today's liberal churches—the gospel is not presented clearly enough for someone to know how to be saved.

The problem is not that the gospel message is complicated or that it requires a theologian to either present or understand it. Rather, it is so simple that a child can grasp it. Neither does the gospel need to be presented in some formulaic way. It can be fully explained in just a couple of minutes in a normal conversation.

And finally, salvation requires more than just mental assent to a certain set of facts or just an intellectual understanding of the gospel—*but it never requires less*. Therefore, the facts of the gospel do need to be presented for someone to be saved.

In his first letter to the church at Corinth, Paul is dealing with a church that apparently has become confused about the simple facts of the gospel, so he explains it very succinctly:

1 Corinthians 15:3–4—

> For I delivered to you first of all that which I also received: that Christ died for our sins according to the Scriptures, and that He was buried, and that He rose again the third day according to the Scriptures.

The Holy Spirit does not operate in a vacuum apart from the presentation of gospel truth.

Romans 10:14–15—

> How then shall they call on Him in whom they have not believed? And how shall they believe in Him of whom they have not heard? And how shall they hear without a preacher? And how shall they preach unless they are sent? As it is written: "How beautiful are the feet of those who preach the gospel of peace, Who bring glad tidings of good things!'"

The Holy Spirit convicts the sinner of the truth of the facts surrounding the gospel and draws the sinner to Christ in the context of that truth.

John 16:8—

> And when He has come, He will convict the world of sin, and of righteousness, and of judgment.

John 6:44—

> No one can come to Me unless the Father who sent Me draws him; and I will raise him up at the last day.

Then in a moment of genuine repentance and faith, by God's grace, the sinner trusts in Christ alone for salvation—for the forgiveness of sin and eternal life.

Acts 16:30–31, 34—

> And he brought them out and said, "Sirs, what must I do to be saved?" So they said, "Believe on the Lord Jesus Christ, and you will be saved, you and your household."
>
> Now when he had brought them into his house, he set food before them; and he rejoiced, having believed in God with all his household.

Romans 10:9–10—

> . . . that if you confess with your mouth the Lord Jesus and believe in your heart that God has raised Him from the dead, you will be saved. For with the heart one believes unto righteousness, and with the mouth confession is made unto salvation.

Ephesians 2:8–9—

> For by grace you have been saved through faith, and that not of yourselves; it is the gift of God, not of works, lest anyone should boast.

It is in that moment that the person is born again and becomes a child of God.

John 1:12–13—

> But as many as received Him, to them He gave the right to become children of God, to those who believe in His name: who were born, not of blood, nor of the will of the flesh, nor of the will of man, but of God.

Of course, there are any number of ways that these essential gospel truths could be presented, even in a novel. But the problem is that in *The Harbinger* virtually none of this is explained in a clear and concise way.

The following is the essence of how Cahn explains what someone must do in order to be born again—to be saved:

[THE PROPHET] "By receiving . . . by letting go . . . by letting the old life end and a new one begin. By choosing . . . by opening your heart to receive that which is beyond containing—the presence . . . the mercy . . . the forgiveness . . . the cleansing . . . the unending love of God."[5]

Unfortunately, the author never explains the meaning of any of this. What does an unbeliever need to do to be saved? Each component of Cahn's answer is followed by a question requiring an answer that *The Harbinger* doesn't supply.

"By receiving . . ." —*But by receiving what?*

"By letting go . . ." —*But by letting go of what?*

"By letting the old life end . . ." —*But how does one do that?*

"By letting . . . a new [life] begin . . ." —*But how does this happen?*

"By choosing . . ." —*But by choosing what?*

"By opening your heart to receive that which is beyond containing" —*But how is an unbeliever supposed to know what this nonsensical statement means?*

"By opening your heart to receive . . . the mercy . . . the forgiveness . . . the cleansing . . . the unending love of God" —*But exactly how does one receive God's mercy, forgiveness, cleansing, and unending love?*

So many words—so little explanation.

Cahn never explains in simple terms what he means by any of this. It's all "Christian-ese" that even many "Christians" would have difficulty explaining very well. Someone with little or no biblical background would not understand at all what The Prophet means when he speaks of *partaking in the infinite sacrifice.*[6]

Not once does the author ever mention the idea of "placing one's faith in Christ" or "believing in Christ" or "trusting in Christ" for one's salvation. In fact, quite inexplicably, the words *faith* and *trust* never appear in relation to salvation or to the gospel anywhere in *The Harbinger.* The word *believe* is used twice in a brief exchange concerning "believing is seeing" versus "seeing is believing," but this is not very helpful the way it is used.[7]

The result is that the gospel is almost completely obscured in the midst of the many words, while the few words and phrases that could have made the gospel very clear are missing. Because of these and other crucial elements of the gospel that are also missing, a genuine concern is whether anyone who does not already understand the gospel could even be saved by reading *The Harbinger*. The problem of sin and judgment is very clear—but the solution is not clear at all.

MISSING ELEMENTS

The deity of Jesus Christ

A central truth of the gospel and one of several that sets biblical Christianity apart from all religions is the deity of Jesus Christ: *Jesus is God*. The author does present the idea in *The Harbinger*, but in only one place in the dialogue, and it is done in a way that could be easily missed or misunderstood by those who are not aware of what the Bible teaches on the matter of Jesus' deity. Nor does Cahn ever use the biblical phrase "Son of God" to refer to Jesus:

> [THE PROPHET] "The giving of Himself . . . God giving Himself to bear the judgment of those under judgment if, by so doing, it would save them. Love puts itself in the place of the other. So then the ultimate manifestation of love would be . . . ."

> [KAPLAN] "God putting Himself in our place."

> [THE PROPHET] "In our life, in our death, in our judgment . . . the sacrifice."

> [KAPLAN] "As in Jesus . . . "[8]

The same dialogue could have made Jesus' identity much more clear with just a couple of minor adjustments. For example:

[THE PROPHET] *"Jesus was more than just a man. He was and is the Son of God—which is another way of saying that He is God. And Jesus, that is to say God Himself, came to bear the judgment of those under judgment . . ."*

[KAPLAN] *"You're saying that Jesus really is God and so God took our judgment in our place?"*

[THE PROPHET] *"Exactly. In our life, in our death, in our judgment . . . the ultimate sacrifice. He died in our place on the cross."*

[KAPLAN] *"So you're saying that Jesus gave Himself as a sacrifice for our sin? For my sin? God Himself took the punishment I deserve? It's unbelievable."*

[THE PROPHET] *"Yes—that's what I'm saying. And we know it is true because this is what God has said in so many places in His Word, the Bible."*

Trying to tell another author how he should write his story may seem rather presumptuous. But that's not what is being suggested. This is just one example of how easy it would have been to add a much-needed extra line or two—just a couple more short phrases. Jesus' identity is a crucial component of the gospel.

The cross of Jesus Christ

One of the more memorable images from Ground Zero in the aftermath of the 9/11 WTC attacks was a remnant of the welded steel superstructure protruding from the rubble to form a twenty-foot high cross. Many took this to be a sign of hope that had been given by God. As seen in the following exchange, Cahn makes it clear that he too personally believes this was a sign from God:

[THE PROPHET] "On the third day after the calamity, a construction worker was standing in the ruins of one of the shattered buildings. When he looked up, he saw it."

[KAPLAN] "The sign . . ."

[THE PROPHET] "The sign . . . unmistakable . . . glaring . . .
forged not by human hands but by the force of the calamity .
. . a cross . . . a perfectly formed cross . . . twenty feet high . . .
of cast iron beams from the fallen towers standing in the midst
of a landscape of devastation . . . as if rising up from the ruins.[9]

Was it a sign from God? Perhaps. No one can really know for sure.
What is known for sure is that people think they see signs from God all the
time, whether in the clouds or on pieces of toast. This isn't meant to mock
the author or anyone else. It seems safe to suggest, however, that very
few of these actually come from God. The Lord has created man with an
exceptional ability to almost instantly perceive order in patterns—whether
they are real or random. Either way, this is not an extremely significant
issue. But there is an issue in all of this that is very significant.

Although Cahn refers to the *Cross at Ground Zero* three times in that
one paragraph, he never makes any connection between it and the Cross
upon which Jesus was crucified. He makes no other mention of the Cross
anywhere in the book. It is never once clearly stated that Jesus died on the
Cross, shedding His blood for the remission of our sins.

The resurrection of Jesus Christ

Jesus' death secured the forgiveness of sin, and His resurrection provides the sure hope of eternal life. Paul makes it clear in 1 Corinthians
15:1-6 that Jesus' resurrection is an essential component of the gospel, and
in Romans 10:9-11 he states that one must believe in His resurrection to
be saved:

1 Corinthians 15:3–8—

For I delivered to you first of all that which I also received: that Christ
died for our sins according to the Scriptures, and that He was buried,
and that He rose again the third day according to the Scriptures, and
that He was seen by Cephas, then by the twelve. After that He was seen
by over five hundred brethren at once, of whom the greater part remain
to the present, but some have fallen asleep. After that He was seen by
James, then by all the apostles. Then last of all He was seen by me also,
as by one born out of due time.

Romans 10:9–11—

> . . . that if you confess with your mouth the Lord Jesus and believe in your heart that God has raised Him from the dead, you will be saved. For with the heart one believes unto righteousness, and with the mouth confession is made unto salvation. For the Scripture says, "Whoever believes on Him will not be put to shame."

There is not the slightest mention of the resurrection of Jesus Christ anywhere in *The Harbinger*. How could this be?

The second coming of Jesus Christ

As previously noted, one of the most important messianic passages in the Bible is found immediately preceding Isaiah 9:10. It promises that Christ will establish an eternal kingdom. Since that kingdom has not yet been established, the problem of not mentioning Jesus' resurrection is compounded by the fact that His return is not mentioned either.

Although Cahn repeatedly emphasizes the danger of God's coming judgment, nowhere does he relate that judgment to the second coming of Christ. Nor does he mention the hope of the peace that will come to the earth during Christ's rule over the promised Millennial kingdom. He comes so close when he refers to Jesus as the Jewish Messiah and the *Hope of Israel*. He comes so close to saying that Israel still has a future. So close.

The testimony of faith in Jesus Christ

In the final chapter of the book, "The Last Seal," Cahn had yet one more opportunity to make it clear that Nouriel Kaplan had been born again through faith in Jesus Christ—but he did not.

Up to this point in the book, Cahn had never used the word *faith* and had never specifically stated that salvation comes through faith in Jesus Christ. However, he wrote the perfect dialogue between Kaplan and Ana Goren, in which he could have naturally included the testimony of a changed life—but he did not.

> [KAPLAN] "Everything would end with eternity—the one thing that wouldn't end, the only thing that would be left when everything else was gone . . . and so the only thing that would matter. I had to get that part right. I had to get my life right with God."

[GOREN] "And did you?"

[KAPLAN] "Yes."

[GOREN] "How?"

[KAPLAN] "By following his words."

[GOREN] "And what happened?"

[KAPLAN] "Everything began to change, not so much around me, not my circumstances, but within. It was a release, a completion, and, for the first time in my life, I had a real peace."

A couple of short sentences. That's all it would have taken. Nothing more.

Kaplan could have so naturally responded to Goren's simple question, "How?"

He could have said something like, "I realized I was a sinful man and that the coming judgment was ultimately about me and about each of us personally. So I placed my faith and trust in Jesus Christ as my Savior, and He completely changed my heart and life forever."

But he did not say it.

CHAPTER 17

THE TENTH SEAL

WHO IS NOURIEL KAPLAN?

IN ADDITION to the nine harbinger seals, there is a tenth, which is Nouriel Kaplan's personal seal. In the last chapter of the book, which deals with the tenth seal, Cahn wraps up the story by further developing Kaplan's character—particularly his role and responsibilities in revealing the hidden mystery of Isaiah 9:10 to the world. This final plot development, combined with what is already known about Kaplan, reveals a significant number of similarities between the main character and the author himself. With so many virtually identical elements, the unmistakable impression is given that this must be by design.

- Just as the author, Kaplan is Jewish.

- Just as the author, Kaplan is from the priestly line of Levi.

- Just as "Cahn" is a Germanized form of the Hebrew word *cohen*, which means priest, "Kaplan" means *chaplain* in German and is thus a translation of *cohen*.[1]

- Just as the author, Kaplan becomes a messianic believer in Christ.

- Just as many are saying of the author, Kaplan has been given a prophetic message by God.

- Just as many are saying of the author, Kaplan is commissioned and anointed to become a prophet himself.

- Just as the author sees himself, Kaplan is to be a "watchman on the wall" to warn of God's impending judgment.

- And just as the author has done, Kaplan is encouraged to get out the message by writing a fictional novel.

It would be difficult to understand all of this as just being a set of unintentional coincidences. As the author notes at the beginning of the book:

"What you are about to read is presented in the form of a story, but what is contained within the story is real."

WHO IS THE PROPHET TO AMERICA?

Clearly Jonathan Cahn develops the character of Nouriel Kaplan in such a way that he shares many identical characteristics with the author himself. However, since the author has revealed what he believes to be previously unseen truth in Isaiah 9:10, there are obvious similarities between Cahn and The Prophet as well. Furthermore, Cahn connects the two characters when The Prophet anoints Nouriel Kaplan for his new role as the next prophet to America.

[THE PROPHET] "So, Nouriel," he said, "do you think you're ready?"

[KAPLAN] "Ready?"

[THE PROPHET] "To fulfill your call."

[KAPLAN] "I don't know, and I have no idea what to do."

[THE PROPHET] "You'll be led, just as you were led to me."

[KAPLAN] "But it's not even my message. It's your message. I'd just be a messenger, a go-between. If they asked me anything about it, I wouldn't know what to say."

[THE PROPHET] "No," he replied, "the message isn't mine. All I am is a messenger, as will be you."

* * *

[THE PROPHET] "How do you think Moses felt when he was called, or Jeremiah . . . or Mary . . . or Peter? Do you think any of them felt remotely adequate? It wasn't about them. And it's not about you. It's about Him. All you have to do is go where He sends you."

[KAPLAN TO GOREN] "Then he reached into his coat and took out a little horn . . . a little ram's horn."

[THE PROPHET] "Close your eyes, Nouriel," he said, lifting the horn above my head.

[KAPLAN TO GOREN] "So I did. I soon felt a thick liquid rolling down my forehead."

[GOREN] "It was oil?" she asked.

[KAPLAN] "Yes, I think olive oil."

[GOREN] "A horn of oil."

[KAPLAN] "The oil of anointing. It was when I felt it running down my cheeks that The Prophet began to pray."

Although Cahn has denied calling himself a prophet, it is a fact that he is considered a modern-day prophet by millions of Americans through radio, television, videos, and his book. By virtue of his silence, Cahn also gave the impression that he accepted Sid Roth's declaration that he is a prophet.

A MYSTERY BEHIND THE ANCIENT MYSTERY?

Jonathan Cahn has over 1,700 of his messages available through the Hope of the World website.[2] The descriptions of many of these messages are quite revealing about his approach to handling the Word of God—which appears to be mystical at its core. The focus of much of his teaching and preaching is apparently the discovery and revelation of mysteries that no one has seen before. His ministry appears to be built around the idea of hidden mysteries exactly like those in *The Harbinger*. The titles and descriptions of just a few of his messages should serve as a warning to any serious student of the Scriptures.

1. MESSIAH'S CATACLYSM & THE HIDDEN WRITINGS OF 30 A.D. (*The amazing signs contained in the hidden writings of the rabbis that happened c. 30 A.D. . . .*)

2. THE COSMIC TSULAV & THE MYSTERY OF PURIM (*The deep mystery at the center of Purim, and the center of the existence itself, the mystery hidden in the Sistine Chapel, Dante's Inferno, Josephus, the Septuagint, and in the ancient Biblical account – the mystery of the Tsulav, the Cross, the Xulon.*)

3. THE SWORD OF AMALEK & THE MYSTERY OF PURIM (*From the day of the Red Sea, Pharaoh's chariots and Amalek, to the Third Reich, Joseph Stalin, Saddam Hussein, and the nuclear sabers of Iran, the amazing mystery of Amalek, the hand of God, and what it has to do with your life.*)

4. THE PRODIGAL SON REVELATION! (*The most universal and personal of Messiah's parables also contains a mystery behind the present age, the Jew, the Gentile, Israel, the Church, and the last days.*)

5. THE MESSIAH BEARER! (*From the deep and mystery filled Book of Hebrews, the mystery of the Messiah Bearer—what it means for your life.*)

6. THE MYSTERY OF THE COSMIC FRINGE (*The Kraspedon Mysteries comes to their conclusion—The mystery of Messiah's sacred garment and the mystery of its fringe and a hint: It has everything to do with you.*)

7. THE NISAN GOSPEL MYSTERY (*All the events of our salvation happened in one single time period – the Biblical month*

of Nisan — Discover the mystery of Nisan, of your salvation, &
the powers you have for breakthrough.)

8. THE COSMIC KEYCHAIN (*As real as a keychain with*
many keys to unlock the doors of a house — there is a supernatu-
ral keychain with supernatural power to unlock the closed doors
of your life.)

9. THE COSMIC KEYCHAIN II (*Messiah has given you a*
keychain with specific powers of breakthrough — learn how to
use the keys & it will change your life.)

10. ENTERING YOUR PROPHETIC DESTINY! (*One of the*
most important and very awesome principles operating in your
life — and how to walk into your prophetic destiny — with some
very cool surprises!)

In the last chapter of the book, Kaplan explains to Goren how he
figured out the meaning of his personal clay seal in what may be a very
revealing exchange. Between the last sentence in the quote below and what
can be seen from the messages above, the real mystery of *The Harbinger*
may be that its foundation is actually Jewish mysticism:

[KAPLAN] "The writing on the seal was in a language I had never
seen before. But I remembered the words of The Prophet that
day we first met on the bench, when he took the seal to examine
it. He said it was Hebrew, but a different form of Hebrew—
Paleo-Hebrew, an older version."

[GOREN] "And did you know anybody who could read Paleo-
Hebrew?"

[KAPLAN] "No. But I knew someone who studied Hebrew from
biblical and rabbinical writings. I looked up the Paleo-Hebrew
alphabet, then transcribed each of the letters into its modern
Hebrew equivalent. Then I made a trip to Brooklyn. That's
where my friend was, an Orthodox Jewish man who ran a little
bookstore, in back of which was a study, a library of all sorts of
mystical Hebrew writings. *That was his passion—finding mean-*
ing in mystical Hebrew literature."

The introduction of Jewish mystical writings into the storyline of *The Harbinger* is very problematic, and one has to wonder why Cahn would have done this.

> Mysticism and mystical experiences have been a part of Judaism since the earliest days. . . . The mystical school of thought came to be know as Kabbalah, from the Hebrew root Qof-Beit-Lamed, meaning "to receive, to accept." The word is usually translated as "tradition."[3]

> "Kabbalah" is a doctrine of esoteric knowledge concerning God and the universe, asserted to have come down as a revelation to the Sages from a remote past, and preserved only by a privileged few. Kabbalah is considered part of the Jewish Oral Law. It is the traditional mystical understanding of the Torah. Kabbalah stresses the reasons and understanding of the commandments, and the cause of events described in the Torah. Kabbalah includes the understanding of the spiritual spheres in creation, and the rules and ways by which God administers the existence of the Universe.[4]

> Most forms of Kabbalah teach that every letter, word, number, and accent of scripture contains a hidden sense; and it teaches the methods of interpretation for ascertaining these occult meanings.[5]

That Cahn would include this reference to Jewish mysticism in the book is not necessarily just an anomaly. Cahn gave a message at his church that also included detailed references to Jewish mystical writings. His message was titled "Gulgatah: The Cosmic Skull: The Rabbinic Mysteries V." The title seems to suggest that this was the fifth in a series of messages on "The Rabbinic Mysteries."

A segment from near the end of this message was uploaded to YouTube on February 25, 2010, and the video is titled, "The Zohar Speaks." This video is connected with the username "bethisraelwayne" which would indicate that the video was uploaded officially by Cahn's church, Jerusalem/Beth Israel Worship Center in Wayne, New Jersey.

The following description accompanies the YouTube video:

"Something never before revealed, to the glory of Messiah! The Cosmic Skull, the mercy of God, and the hidden and mystical writings of the Rabbis that point to Messiah."[6] The description coincides exactly with the overall trajectory of Cahn's messages, and that of *The Harbinger*, which is to reveal to the world mysteries that have been hidden until he discovers and proclaims them.

The Judaism 101 website notes the following concerning the Zohar:

> In the middle ages, many of these mystical teachings were committed to writing in books like the Zohar. Many of these writings were asserted to be secret ancient writings or compilations of secret ancient writings.[7]

Even though he introduces the Zohar as a "hostile witness," the way Cahn describes its teachings gives the impression that he views the Zohar as being a credible source of truth as held by the ancient rabbis:

> Incredible thing. Blew me away. I found it in the mystical Jewish writings of the Zohar. Something I never heard mentioned anywhere, ever. . . . The Zohar speaks, the rabbis are writing of the redemption of the world with Messiah's coming. They speak of life from the dead. They speak of resurrection, the redemption of the world. . . . They say it all will come, the power of all this, the miracle of all this will come from a sacred thing, a sacred place. And this place, this thing, is where all the mercy of God is stored. All the mercy of God pours out from this place, this thing. What is it? Very strange. They call it the "gulgatah." This holy, mystical thing. . . . The most famous scene in human history, the center of salvation. Messiah dying on that hill which appears as a skull. That's why they called it "gulgatah"—Golgatha. And which signifies God's mercy. All His mercy. Why on earth would the rabbis put it there? Makes no sense at all—except that God just puts it in.[8]

"God just puts it in." In other words, God inspired the rabbis to write about redemption coming from a skull, yet they had no idea what it meant. So, in this message Cahn presents concepts that are reflected in *The Harbinger*. The first is that Isaiah 9:10 contains a mystery that no one has seen before—Cahn has discovered it for the very first time—just as he has discovered this inspired message in the ancient rabbinic writings. The second is that Tom Daschle was inspired by God to proclaim America's defiance and thus set up the nation for judgment—even though he didn't know what he was doing—just as is true of the ancient rabbis.

As Cahn continues his exposition of the Zohar, the mystical nature of his thinking becomes even more clear. And once again he notes that perhaps no one has ever said the words he has just uttered:

> In the gulgatah—Golgotha—sit thousands of myriads of worlds. And from the gulgatah—Golgotha—drips dew and fills . . . the dew fills the world and the dead will awaken in the world to come as the dew comes forth. The dew is the light of the ancient one. The light of the ancient one comes from Golgotha and as it touches—the dead ones come to life. From Golgotha is the light of God bringing life from the dead. Golgotha—the radiance of God which brings life. Whoa! That's amazing stuff. And that may be the first time it's ever been said. 'Cause you have to be a believer and you have to be in that stuff.[9]

What stuff? The ancient mystical writings. Yet even more telling is that Cahn confidently elevates the rabbis to the level of Moses and Daniel.

> The death of Messiah—all pinpointed in time and space. Moses zeroed in on the day. Passover. He dies on the day that the lamb is killed. The prophets—Daniel zeroes in on the time period, mathematically, before 70 A.D. Daniel—those seventy sevens. The rabbis in the book of Moed, unwittingly, and another thing we shared this [sic], zeroed in on the year by saying that the cosmic change all took place in the year 30 A.D. . . . And now the very hill, the very place, here in, of all places, the rabbinical writings, the Zohar. . . . you want mercy, you go there. Listen to the rabbis on this point. . . . [10]

How can a pastor instruct his congregation to "listen to the rabbis" who produced the Zohar and tell them these rabbis were inspired by God? The Zohar is not simply an innocuous source of information—it is an extrabiblical guide to "higher spirituality." It is mystical. It is occult.

> The Zohar cannot be understood and felt directly, but requires preconception of spirituality, before one approaches the book.

The greatest Kabbalist of our time—Rabbi Yehuda Ashlag (Baal HaSulam)—wrote introductions to The Zohar precisely to guide one's approach to this profound book prior to studying it.

Such articles cultivate one's spiritual qualities to perceive the Higher reality. Additionally, these texts provide knowledge of how to approach certain terms, phrases, and concepts in The Zohar, to maximize its use as a guide for spiritual attainment, avoiding being lost in materialized depictions that the human mind is prone to form.[11]

In the July 3, 2012, interview when Brannon Howse expressed his deep concern about Cahn using mystical sources for his messages, Cahn tried to justify his practice by noting that the Apostle Paul also referred to the teaching of pagan philosophers in his address to the Athenians (Acts 17:22-31). He went on to suggest that Paul would have been "crucified" by discernment ministries for using a hymn to Zeus and because of his associations.[12]

That is a red herring. The two situations are completely different. Paul's approach is nothing like Cahn's. Cahn refers to the mystical rabbinical writings positively, saying that because God had inspired them his church should "listen to the rabbis." He presents the Zohar as something that can be studied and its depths plumbed for hidden mysteries like he has just revealed for the first time.

In stark contrast, Paul immediately tells his audience that what they have been taught by their poets about the unknown god they worship is completely wrong. He does not suggest that their sayings contain hidden mysteries that were inspired by God and that he had just discovered for the first time. Paul never implies that the Athenians should listen to these men. Rather he refers to a single point of agreement (we all come from God) to denounce their idols. From Romans we understand that the knowledge of that truth is not a hidden mystery but has rather been made plain to everyone through both the conscience and the Creation (Romans 1:18-2:16).

Lest someone think this too was just an anomaly, another message from Cahn was uploaded to YouTube by user "bethisraelwayne" on April 10, 2012: "Messiah's Cosmic Cataclysm and the Hidden Writings of 30 A.D." This video includes the following description:

The amazing signs contained in the hidden writings of the rabbis that happened c. 30 A.D., the Scarlet Chord [sic], the Lots of Scapegoat, the Western Light, the Exile of the Sanhedrin, the Doors of the Temple, and the cataclysmic power of the Lamb—Great for believer and unbeliever alike.[13]

The following excerpts from that message confirm his belief in the significance and authority of the extra-biblical writings of the rabbis as found in the book of Yoma in the Babylonian Talmud:

But now could there be any other witness, historical witnesses, even beyond the gospel accounts—that confirm something cataclysmic happened. The answer is amazingly, "Yes!" And just as amazingly it comes from people who oppose the faith—so it's even more powerful a witness. The Talmud consists of the writings of the rabbis—the rabbis who did not believe in Yeshua, Jesus as the Messiah. . . . The earliest writings or the earliest notes are based on the writings, accounts from the time of Messiah. . . . And one of those books is called the book of Yoma, in the Talmud. Orthodox Jews read this book. Yoma 39a. The rabbis record a phenomenom [sic]—strange events that take place in the temple of Jerusalem. Signs. Events of such significance they deemed it worthy of recording it in the closest thing they had after the Scriptures.[14]

Cahn goes on to explain that the rabbis taught that a miracle took place such that the center lamp of the menorah in the temple never went out even when the oil in the other six lamps was used up. Then, in 30 A.D. the miracle ceased, coinciding with the death of the Messiah.

So in the temple of Jerusalem they kept the menorah, the seven-branched candlestick. . . . a symbol of the light of God. . . . by tradition the central lamp was the westernmost lamp that lit up all the other ones. . . . It kept burning even when the other ones would go out. . . . The rabbis noted this was a sign. . . . They said it was a sign of the glory of God . . . but the rabbis record something happened . . . that had to do with Israel's light—the menorah, the flame. . . . The rabbis record all of a sudden the western light, this key light, stopped shining. . . . and they view it as a cosmic change.[15]

Cahn appears to uncritically accept the writings of the Talmud concerning this miracle, even though there is no scriptural support, and presents it to his congregation as absolute fact. In this eight-minute segment of the message, he also refers to other miracles associated with the temple service in 30 A.D.

Perhaps such miracles did occur, but without scriptural support, there is no way to know for certain. At best, this account makes for an interesting historical footnote, but it cannot be treated as factual in the way that Cahn has. There is no way to know what really happened and there is no way to know that this was not simply a Jewish myth.

Unfortunately, this treatment of the rabbinic material is consistent with Cahn's frequent practice of "discovering and revealing" hidden mysteries—be it in the Bible or in extrabiblical Jewish writings like the Talmud or even in mystical kabbalistic writings like the Zohar. Although it seems unlikely that Cahn would subscribe to classic Jewish mysticism, as a messianic rabbi he certainly seems to have developed his own variation.

Have untold numbers of Christians unwittingly accepted mystical Jewish thought? And after having done so, how may pastors, teachers, and other ministry leaders have preached messages connected to the claims of *The Harbinger* and have publicly endorsed, promoted, and defended the book and Jonathan Cahn? How many have shared this book and the documentary with unbelieving family and friends? How many millions of dollars have gone into keeping *The Harbinger* on so many best-seller lists, including at or near the top of the theology category on Amazon.com for weeks?

Something seems to be very wrong.

CHAPTER 18

FINAL THOUGHTS

JONATHAN CAHN'S intention is for *The Harbinger* to be a powerful wake-up call for America—a call to repent from her rapid descent into the depths of sin and turn to God as her only hope of avoiding His imminent judgment. The author has explicitly warned that failure to do so puts the United States on a direct collision course with the same devastation faced by ancient Israel, who in arrogance and pride refused to heed the warnings of the prophets. Cahn argues that God has already warned America twice with the terrorist attacks of 9/11/2001 and the financial calamities of 2008 and beyond. Whatever else may be problematic concerning the rest of the book, he is absolutely correct in his assessment that America is in serious spiritual trouble.

His message is timely, given everything that is going on in the United States with the upcoming presidential election, the Occupy Wall Street Movement, the astronomical debt, ongoing racial tensions, illegal immigration issues, high unemployment, economic hardships, the gay rights movement, and a virtually endless list of moral and ethical issues. Then there are the international problems of al Qaeda and terrorism, Afghanistan and Pakistan, Iraq, Iran, Syria, the Israel/Palestinian issue, Hamas, Hezbollah, the Muslim Brotherhood, the Arab Spring, China, North Korea, Russia, Venezuela, and the list goes on.

Cahn has grabbed the attention of millions—and he has struck a nerve. He has also brought it to his readers' attention that the real danger faced by each of them is ultimately a deeply personal spiritual matter. The *Day of*

Judgment for a nation has temporal consequences, but for each individual the consequences are eternal. For those who have taken this idea seriously, we can praise and thank the Lord for His gracious loving-kindness.

DOES THE END JUSTIFY THE MEANS?

Jonathan Cahn could have communicated what he believes is his real message in any number of ways, including through a fictional novel. The main problem is not that he uses fiction as his genre of choice. Rather, the real problem arises from the way he has tried to achieve his goals. His ends, as important as they are, do not justify the means he has employed to accomplish them at so many points along the way.

Cahn has departed from a literal, grammatical, historical hermeneutic in favor of looking for hidden mysteries while engaging in allegorical interpretation and untenable speculation. In short, he has mishandled the Word of God.

The manipulation of both biblical and historical evidence reveals a sensational "connect-the-dots" approach to understanding and linking the prophetic Word of God and current events. A pattern of both overstating his case and misleading the reader through a very selective use of facts and figures quickly emerges as *The Harbinger*'s foundation.

In spite of the way it may appear to some, Jonathan Cahn's motives are not being questioned. This response to *The Harbinger* is not an indictment of Cahn's heart. When words like "misleading" and "manipulation" are used, they refer only to the appearance and the result. This book is exclusively about the "what" and the "how"—never the "why." There is no intention to deal with what is the purview of God alone. Only those things that can be verified have been presented, and even then not as any sort of judgment of the man and his character.

ANTICIPATED OPPOSITION

In one of the last exchanges in the book between Nouriel Kaplan and The Prophet, it is clear that Cahn anticipated opposition to the book and included a sort of a "preemptive strike" against his critics:

[KAPLAN] "They'll do everything they can to attack and discredit it."

[THE PROPHET] "Of course they will," he said. "Otherwise they'd have to accept it."

[KAPLAN] "But not only the message."

[THE PROPHET] "No, the messenger as well."

[KAPLAN] "They'll do everything they can to attack and discredit the one who bears the message."

[THE PROPHET] "Yes," said the prophet. "The messenger will be opposed, vilified and hated, mocked and slandered. It has to be that way, just as it was for Jeremiah and Baruch."[1]

One of the most obvious possible groups of critics would include those who identify themselves as religious Christians but who also have a liberal theology that doesn't take the Bible seriously nor has much of anything biblical to say about sin, judgment, wrath, or hell. Given the popularity of the book and their apparent silence, it seems possible that Cahn may have gotten through to a segment of that demographic. If some in this group have been challenged to reconsider their views, that would be a positive thing.

A second group could conceivably be those politicians whom Cahn indicted for quoting Isaiah 9:10 and those who frequently repeated the words, "We will rebuild." His suggestion that they were pronouncing God's judgment on America is not one that any of them could be too happy with. However, the silence from this group, as well, would seem to indicate that either they don't know about the book yet or have just chosen to ignore it.

Overall, given the number and nature of the problems throughout *The Harbinger*, the book and its author have actually received surprisingly little criticism. Even though it isn't unusual for books with demonstrable hermeneutical issues and questionable theology to become best sellers in the broader Christian market, the popularity of *The Harbinger* even in evangelical circles has been quite unusual.

A historically strong commitment to the inspiration, inerrancy, authority, and sufficiency of the Word of God has served to guard conservative evangelicals from falling victim to unbiblical interpretations, aberrant theology, and dangerous philosophies. The commitment to a literal, grammatical, historical hermeneutic has been the glue that has generally held everyone together when these problematic teachings have come along.

For some reason, though, *The Harbinger* has elicited a much different and divided reaction among evangelicals than would normally happen. This has included division among pastors, theologians, Bible teachers, ministry leaders, and those in the pews. Quite unexpectedly, the division has occurred among some who have consistently stood together on many such issues over the years.

Although praise of *The Harbinger* has come from across an extremely broad theological spectrum, the comparatively little criticism the book has received has been from a relatively small group who share a clear set of mutually held biblical and theological commitments.

Among those who love *The Harbinger* and have vigorously promoted and defended Jonathan Cahn, the book has in many ways become a rallying point, a theological bridge, and common ground as no other issue in recent memory.

Among those who have serious concerns about *The Harbinger* and Cahn's views, the common ground they share is not their opposition to the book, but rather a firm commitment to a biblical hermeneutic, as well as the theology and view of the prophetic Scriptures that flow from that. This is not to suggest that none of *The Harbinger*'s supporters share this same biblical commitment—undoubtedly many do. So, for those who do, what is at the heart of such sharp differences?

SOURCES OF DIFFERENCES

Those who have opposed *The Harbinger* tend to uniformly do so on the basis of a number of factors. One major concern is that *The Harbinger* gives the distinct (and wrong) impression that America has been elevated to a status in God's program that has been reserved for Israel alone. This impression is deepened, at least in part, due to what is seen as a problem with the hermeneutical principles used to interpret Isaiah 9:10 (and the Old Testament in general). This has led to further concerns about how passages that were given specifically to Israel have been applied to New Testament believers, as well as to the United States, which is a Gentile nation. Ultimately, this has resulted in differences between the two sides over the correlation and application of Isaiah 9:10 and other passages to recent events going back to September 2001 and even back to the founding of America. *The Harbinger*'s supporters do not seem to share these concerns.

Further differences have included (but aren't limited to) concerns about the sometimes selective and misleading use of historical facts and data, hints of the apparent influence of Jewish mysticism on Cahn's theology and methodology, the view among extreme Charismatics that Cahn is a modern-day prophet, discrepancies between what Cahn has written and what he has said in various interviews, and a number of other issues.

When everything is considered, it seems very clear to those who have been critical of *The Harbinger* that the book is not a prophetic message from God and needs to be rejected in spite of its call to repentance. On the other hand, *The Harbinger*'s proponents believe that God has uniquely used Jonathan Cahn to write this book "for such a time as this" and that in spite of whatever flaws it may have, its message needs to be embraced wholeheartedly.

THE REAL TRAGEDY

In the final analysis, even with its core message of repentance, *The Harbinger*'s phenomenal success is the result of a tragedy whose magnitude can be measured in any number of many ways. It can be measured in terms of dollars and the hundreds of thousands of copies that have been sold since its release. It can also be measured in terms of *The Harbinger*'s long-held position near the top of the theology category on Amazon.com and in terms of the large number of positive comments and reviews it has received across the Internet. Or it can be measured in terms of the millions of television viewers and radio listeners who have been dramatically influenced through the interviews Jonathan Cahn has given.

The real tragedy is what ultimately allowed this to happen—or perhaps more precisely, what *caused* this to happen. *The Harbinger*'s popularity and success can be attributed to essentially the same factors that have driven the success of other books that also have serious hermeneutical and theological problems. We aren't too surprised when this happens among those who have long since abandoned the practice of biblical discernment. The difference this time around is the wide-spread acceptance of *The Harbinger* by so many evangelical believers—who, as a group, historically have been so much more careful.

As evangelicals, we have been known for our knowledge of and commitment to the full counsel of God. As individual believers, evangelicals have been known by the desire to search out a matter, comparing Scripture with Scripture. We have been willing to do any other research necessary to thoroughly examine an issue for ourselves—particularly when the propositions and claims are as far-reaching as those in *The Harbinger*. Then, if needed, we have taken a stand and warned others of the potential dangers of a given teaching, trend, or movement. Historically, this has set us apart from all others who would identify themselves as Christians.

Unfortunately, a growing segment of the evangelical church seems to be losing its way when it comes to discernment. Statistics indicate that fewer and fewer self-identified born-again believers hold to a biblical view of the inspiration, inerrancy, authority, and sufficiency of Scripture. This inevitably has a direct impact on the average Christian's ability to discern false teaching when it arises, especially within the church, where it is often the most subtle and insidious.

Another major problem is that over the last two decades especially, a philosophy of ministry has developed that has radically de-emphasized biblical exposition and the importance of sound doctrine. Far too many have adopted the mantra, "Doctrine divides, but love unites" when the biblical truth is that doctrine divides because belief unites.

With the proliferation of books and blogs, we have become far too dependent on what others are writing when it comes to our own understanding of the Word of God. With ubiquitous access to streaming audio and video, we have become far too dependent on what others are saying when it comes to our own spiritual well-being and maturity. We're letting others do the "heavy lifting" while we sit, watch, listen, and atrophy.

One result of this is personality-driven division in the church—just as it was in the Corinthian church, with some saying, "I am of Paul" or "I am of Apollos," while others say, "I am of Peter," and still others declare, "I am of Christ."[2] That there is any controversy at all surrounding *The Harbinger* should be setting off all sorts of alarms because this isn't that difficult. That we're even debating this book suggests that we're in deeper trouble than many of us would have thought when it comes to searching the Scriptures "to find out whether these things are so."[3]

Those of us with concerns about *The Harbinger* are in the minority, but we shouldn't be. *The Harbinger* is a classic case study in precisely how not to handle, how not to interpret, and how not to apply the Word of God. For this reason, all of us should be very concerned that so many have gotten it wrong with this book. The warning signs are many, and most are in plain view, requiring just a little work to cut through the fog.

For example, one of Cahn's goals is to persuade the reader that the biblical aspects of *The Harbinger* are based on sound hermeneutics and the proper interpretation of the Word of God. At first glance, this may appear to be the case because he does present quite a bit of historical context (albeit much of that is problematic, as well). Consequently it would seem that many otherwise diligent believers may have let their guard down. Many seem to have missed the fact that Cahn has lifted Isaiah 9:10 entirely out of its literary context—to which the historical context must always be the servant.

He fails to discuss, mention, or even allude to the verses that precede the passage in question—which include one of the most significant Christological and Messianic Kingdom passages in the entire Old Testament. If for no other reason than this, mature believers should walk away from *The Harbinger*. We cannot correctly understand and we cannot correctly apply the Word of God apart from the context. As has been said so many times, "The context isn't the main thing—it's the only thing."

As another example, the book conveys what Cahn claims is a prophetic message. Yet *The Harbinger* clearly does not meet the requirements for a word from God. It is filled with theological, logical, and historical problems, as has been shown throughout this book. It claims that God has done things that He hasn't done and that He has revealed things that are demonstrably not true.

The Harbinger purports to demonstrate that an array of historical facts, when taken together, unmistakably point to the hand of God. Yet, because of the misleading way in which Cahn handles so many of those facts, it falls far short of achieving that goal. He raises speculation to the level of fact and connects dots that just aren't there. He very selectively picks and chooses what information he uses, while ignoring that which would otherwise undermine his argument. We can never let these kinds of things slip by us.

Most troubling of all is that so little is said about Christ and His work. And what is said is unacceptably vague or incomplete. How could a post-resurrection prophet of God fail to mention the resurrection—apart from which there is no gospel at all?

Significantly, one of the most succinct and clear presentations of the gospel in the entire New Testament is found in 1 Corinthians chapter 15—the very chapter in which Paul takes the Corinthians to task because some in the church were even denying the resurrection. Cahn certainly does not deny the resurrection, yet inexplicably he has left it out of his book.

As it is, between this problem and that of being very vague about the Cross, he utterly fails to present the gospel clearly enough for someone to know how to be saved. He never mentions that salvation is a free gift of God, which is received by faith. How could so many have missed this glaring omission—or let it slide, if they did notice?

The Harbinger repeatedly issues a call to repentance in the face of impending judgment—which is all well and good. Yet, even if we believe the office of prophet still exists today, how could The Prophet, in this context, fail to mention the coming judgments and the return of Christ foretold in the book of Revelation?

Like a beautiful piece of furniture that appears to be handcrafted from the finest oak but really has only the very thinnest of oak veneers, *The Harbinger* has only a veneer that gives it the appearance of being biblical. How could so many believers be deceived by this? Is it because the church has largely abdicated its responsibility to examine and test a matter in light of Scripture?

The Harbinger has mesmerized a disproportionately large number within our ranks. Has Cahn, wittingly or unwittingly, created an illusion so elaborate and stunning—an illusion so effective—that many have actually become deluded by what they *think* they see? What *The Harbinger* presents as facts and truth is not reality. There needs to be a "reveal." The curtain needs to be pulled back. The book needs to be examined from another angle—the biblical angle. Its claims need to be tested, especially the foundational claim that someone has discovered an ancient mystery in Isaiah 9:10, a mystery so well hidden that it has eluded everyone—until now. We all share this responsibility.

Much of the church today seems to be well on its way to embracing the same apostasy that plagued Corinth and so many other churches by the end of the first century. In the early chapters of the book of Revelation, the risen Savior, in all His exalted glory, chastised five of the seven churches in Asia Minor. He chastised the churches—the fellowships of believers—that had failed to remain faithful to Him and to His word.

Arrayed in the blazing white light of His righteousness, Christ declared such things as "I have this against you. . . . Repent, or else I will come to you quickly. . . . All the churches shall know that I am He who searches the minds and hearts. . . . If you will not watch, I will come upon you as a thief. . . . Because you are lukewarm, and neither cold nor hot, I will vomit you out of my mouth."

Warning the church at Ephesus, He cautioned:

Revelation 2:5—

Remember therefore from where you have fallen; repent and do the first works, or else I will come to you quickly and remove your lampstand from its place—unless you repent.

Thirty years earlier, the Apostle Peter had put it this way:

1 Peter 4:17—

For the time has come for judgment to begin at the house of God; and if it begins with us first, what will be the end of those who do not obey the gospel of God?

The Harbinger is neither the first, nor will it be the last, to put believers to the test. When all the hype has faded, and the book has quietly slipped off the best-seller lists, inevitably there will be another test to take *The Harbinger*'s place. There will be yet another challenge to examine the

Scriptures to see if these things are so—and another *opportunity* for us to uphold the final authority of the Word of God—just as good students of the Bible have always done.

We are reminded of Luke's account of what happened in Berea, when Paul first went to the synagogues to proclaim the gospel to the Jews:

Acts 17:11—

> These were more fair-minded than those in Thessalonica, in that they received the word with all readiness, and searched the Scriptures daily to find out whether these things were so.

Their approach became the model for examining any and all claims that a message is from God. And their approach was the key to what ultimately happened in that city:

Acts 17:12—

> Therefore many of them believed, and also not a few of the Greeks, prominent women as well as men.

What Next?

So, what will we now do with *The Harbinger*?

Will the author reconsider what he has written and said? Will those who have embraced the book reconsider their position? Will everyone step back, take a deep breath, and re-examine *The Harbinger* in the light of the truth of Scripture and the facts of history? Will we put *The Harbinger* to the test, or will we continue to allow it to test us and our commitment to handle the Word of God with integrity?

Will we take to heart and learn from Paul's example as he exhorted the believers in Corinth when we hear the teaching of others and as we ourselves teach the Scriptures?

2 Corinthians 4:1–2—

> Therefore, since we have this ministry, as we have received mercy, we do not lose heart. But we have renounced the hidden things of shame, not walking in craftiness nor handling the word of God deceitfully, but by manifestation of the truth commending ourselves to every man's conscience in the sight of God.

By the grace of God, and with the help of His Spirit, we can—and we must.

* * *

ENDNOTES

CHAPTER 1

1. Jonathan Cahn is the senior pastor of Jerusalem/Beth Israel Worship Center in Wayne, New Jersey. On the church's website, it is suggested that Beth Israel is perhaps the largest messianic congregation in the United States. He is generally referred to as "Rabbi."

2. In Cahn's book, "The Prophet" is not capitalized, but it is capitalized here and throughout for clarity.

3. Jonathan Cahn, *The Harbinger* (Lake Mary, FL: Frontline, Charisma Media/Charisma House Book Group, 2011), v.

4. Ibid., back cover.

5. Ibid., 22.

6. Ibid., 227.

7. Reader reviews of *The Harbinger*, amazon.com website, accessed June 2, 2012, http://www.amazon.com/the-harbinger-ancient-mystery-Americas/dp/161638610X /ref=sr_1?ie=UTF8&qid=1332454190 &sr=8-1.

8. Pat Robertson, interview with Jonathan Cahn on *The 700 Club*, January 3, 2012, http://www.cbn.com/media/player/index.aspx?s=/mp4/SUB109_JonathanCahn _010312_WS.

9. Jeff Danelek, "Top 10 Most Remarkable Coincidences in History," http://www.top tenz.net/top-10-most-remarkable-coincidences-in-history.php.

10. Ibid.

CHAPTER 2

1. Discussion between Jonathan Cahn and David James moderated by Jimmy DeYoung on *Prophecy Today*, recorded April 4, 2012 and released April 6, 2012, http://resource.prophecytoday.com/2012/04/special-interview-with-author-of.html.

2. It is beyond the scope of this book to argue for or against what is known as *sensus plenior* ("fuller sense").

3. Cahn, *Harbinger*, 61.

4. Ibid., 3.

CHAPTER 3

1. Cahn, *Harbinger*, 49.

2. Ibid.

3. Ibid.

4. Jonathan Cahn, interview by Jim and Lori Bakker, *Jim Bakker Show*, April 30, 2012, http://www.youtube.com/watch?v=8OxxSOZdPhk.

CHAPTER 4

1. Discussion Cahn/James, *Prophecy Today*, (first question at the 20:45 mark, second question at the 32:05 mark).

2. Jonathan Cahn, interview by Brannon Howse, *Worldview Weekend*, aired July 3, 2012, http://www.worldviewweekend.com/worldview-radio/play.php?id=showsFlat-21564 (at the 6:34 mark).

3. Jonathan Cahn interview by Molly Noble Bull, Commandment Keepers website, May 13, 2012, http://commandmentkeepers.com/?p=1755.

4. Promotional copy from *It's Supernatural*, https://secure2.convio.net/srmv/site/Ecommerce?VIEW_PRODUCT=true&product_id=18302&store_id=1101&JServSessionIdr004=p31kyw8u23.app227a.

5. Promotional copy for *The Harbinger/Isaiah 9:10 Prophecy*, http://www.theharbinger-jonathancahn.com/Condensed_DVD_Set.

6. Promotional copy for *The Isaiah 9:10 Prophecy*, http://www.youtube.com/watch?v=DGxvfgHSAFY.

7. Promotional copy for *The Harbinger*, http://www.amazon.com/The-harbinger-ancient-mystery-Americas/dp/161638610X/ref=sr_1_1?ie=UTF8&qid=1332907071&sr=8-1.

8. Sid Roth, in an interview with Jonathan Cahn, *It's Supernatural*, September 19-25, 2011, http://www.sidroth.org/site/News2?page=NewsArticle&id=10457&news_iv_ctrl=0&abbr=tv_ (at the 8:21 mark).

9. Roth, *Supernatural*, (at the 22:12 mark).

10. *Isamu and Paul Show*, YouTube channel, http://www.youtube.com/watch?v=nCNRM8Fzji8&feature=related.

11. "A Call to Repentance," Crossroad Community website, http://ccbutler.org/cultureofhonor/a-call-to-repentance/.

12. Jennifer LeClaire, "Great Judgment, Great Awakening...or Both?" reprinted on CharismaNews.com opinion page, http://charismanews.com/index.php/search/?searchword=Jonathan%20Cahn&areas[0]=gitags.

13. Jennifer LeClaire, "Print Great Judgment, Great Awakening...Or Both?" ministry website, April 28, 2012, http://www.jenniferleclaire.org/articles/entry/print-great-judgment-great-awakening-...-or-both.

CHAPTER 5

1. David Wilkerson (5/19/31-4/27/11) was the founder of the addiction recovery program Teen Challenge and founding pastor of Times Square Church in New York City.

2. Gene – A Prophet, blog entry, "David Wilkerson's The Vision reviewed yet again," http://prophetgene.blogspot.com/2010/04/david-wilkersons-vision-reviewed-yet.html.

3. David Wilkerson, "Prophetic Message to New York," September 7, 1992, http://www.scribd.com/doc/16783193/DAVID-WIKERSON-Prophetic-Message-to-New-York-2.

4. David Wilkerson, "The Solomon Church," December 19, 1994, http://www.world challenge.org/en/node/4213.

5. Jonathan Cahn, interview by Sid Roth, *It's Supernatural*, September 26-October 2, 2011, http://www.sidroth.org/site/News2?abbr=tv_&page=NewsArticle&id=10494 (at the 2:32 mark).

6. Jonathan Cahn, interview by Pat Robertson, *The 700 Club*, January 3, 2012, http://www.cbn.com/media/player/index.aspx?s=/mp4/SUB109_JonathanCahn_010312_WS.

7. Wilkerson, "Prophetic Message."

8. Ron McKenzie, Kingdom Watcher website, http://www.kingwatch.co.nz/Prophetic_Ministry/testing_ prophets.htm.

9. David Wilkerson, "The Reproach of the Solemn Assembly," audio sermon, 55 min., http://media.sermonindex.net/0/SID0225.mp3.

10. "Chuck Pierce: Celebrate Passover," The Elijah List website, March 2, 2012, http://www.elijahlist.com/words/display_word.html?ID=10772.

11. Jonathan Cahn, "Response from Jonathan Cahn/In-Depth," http://thethings2come.org/?p-506.

12. Ibid.

13. *Jim Bakker Show*, April 30, 2012, http://jimbakkershow.com/video/show-2054/.

14. Ibid., (at the 5:15 mark).

CHAPTER 6

1. Any statement attributed to Jonathan Cahn for which there is no specific citation in this review comes from a discussion between Cahn and myself, which was moderated by Jimmy DeYoung and recorded on April 4, 2012. It is available for listening or download at: http://resource.prophecytoday.com/2012/04/special-interview-with-author-of.html.

2. Cahn, *Harbinger*, v.

3. Ibid., 8-9.

CHAPTER 7

1. Cahn, *Harbinger*, 3.
2. Ibid., 18-19.
3. Ibid., 38.
4. Ibid., 61.
5. Ibid., 104.
6. Ibid., 109.
7. Ibid., 195.
8. Ibid., 141.
9. Cahn, Robertson, *700 Club*, (at the 2:15 mark).

CHAPTER 8

1. Cahn, *Harbinger*, 18-19.
2. Gavin Finley, M.D., "The Puritan Belief in 'One Nation Under God,'" http://endtimepilgrim.org/puritans04.htm.
3. Ibid.
4. Brandon Vallorani, "Advancing the Kingdom – in God's Strength or Our Own?" August 15, 2011, http://postmillennialism.com/2011/08/advancing-the-kingdom—in-god's-strength-or-our-own/.
5. Finley, "Puritan Belief."
6. Cahn, interview by Bull.
7. Cahn, *Harbinger*, 18-19.
8. The British-Israel-World Federation, "Our History," http://www.britishisrael.co.uk/history.php.
9. In the decade following the death of Herbert Armstrong (the founder), the leadership began to recognize the denomination's serious doctrinal errors, including the belief in Anglo-Israelism. Because of the radical theological changes, in 1997 it was accepted as a member of the National Association of Evangelicals and in 2009 changed the name to Grace Communion International. http://www.gci.org/aboutus/history.
10. Glenn Beck, interview with Timothy Ballard, May 17, 2012, http://www.glennbeck.com/2012/05/17/american-covenant-glenn-interviews-author-timothy-ballard/.
11. Glenn Beck an Unlikely Mormon, unofficial fan page, http://glennbeckmormon.com/.
12. Digital Legend website, Timothy Ballard bio, http://www.digitalegend.com/catalog/index.php?cPath=33.
13. Timothy Ballard, *The Covenant: America's Sacred and Immutable Connection to Ancient Israel* (Kindle Locations 619-622), Legends Library, Kindle edition, (2012-05-16).
14. Glenn Beck, radio broadcast, May 29, 2012, http://web.gbtv.com/media/video.jsp?content_ id=21859995&topic_id=23419450&v=3.

15. Glenn Beck, GBTV broadcast, http://www.youtube.com/watch?v= _Q8kcEmSn2U&feature=relate.

16. Glenn Beck, GBTV broadcast, http://www.youtube.com/watch?v=Ci2bl1U5c-U (at the 7:55 mark).

17. Ibid.

18. Ibid.

19. Cahn, "Response from/In-Depth."

20. The Foundation for Indigenous Research and Mormonism, Spring 2012 Conference, speaker bio, http://events.r20.constantcontact.com/register/event?llr=z7 h5t5cab&oeidk=a07e5jzb6k9f53a3108.

21. That includes all of Israel from both Northern and Southern Kingdoms.

22. Cahn, *Harbinger*, 219-20.

23. Jonah 3.

24. Genesis, chapters 12, 13, 15, 17, 22; Deuteronomy 30; 2 Samuel 7; Jeremiah 31 (with various aspects and additional confirmations in other verses).

CHAPTER 9

1. Cahn, *Harbinger*, 118, 232 ("Messiah" is from the Hebrew for anointed one just as "Christ" is from the Greek form of the same term.).

2. Ibid., 174.

3. Mike Shuster, "Iran's President Renews Interest in 'Hidden Imam,'" *Morning Edition*, NPR, May 30, 2006, http://www.npr.org/templates/story/storyphp?storyid=5438641.

4. John von Heyking, "Iran's President and the Politics of the Twelfth Imam," guest commentary, Ashland University, Ashbrook Center for Public Affairs, November 2005, http://www.ashbrook.org/publicat/guest/05/vonheyking/twelfthimam.html.

5. 1 Thessalonians 4:13-18; 1 Corinthians 15:22-44.

6. Daniel 9:20-27.

7. Matthew 24-25; 2 Thessalonians 2:1-12; Revelation 4-19.

8. Revelation 19-20.

9. Discussion Cahn/James, *Prophecy Today*.

ENDNOTES

CHAPTER 10

1. Cahn, *Harbinger*, 9.

2. Mark Hosenball, "U.S. has 55 daily encounters with 'suspected terrorists,'" Reuters, May 15, 2012, http://ca.news.yahoo.com/u-55-daily-encounters-suspected-terrorists -222758155--finance.html.

3. "Seward's Folly, the Purchase of Alaska," U.S. History website page, http:// www.u-s-history.com/pages/h230.html.

4. R. Taylor, "The Capture of Detroit 1812," War of 1812 website, http://www .warof1812.ca/batdetroit.html.

5. "The British Burn Washington, DC, 1814," EyeWitness to History website, http:// eyewitnesstohistory.com/washingtonsack.htm.

6. "Terrorist Attacks in the U.S. or Against Americans," Infoplease website, http:// www.infoplease.com/ipa/0001454.html.

7. Ibid.

8. Ibid.

9. Cahn, *Harbinger*, 38.

10. "Osama bin Laden, A Chronology of His Political Life," from the documentary "Hunting bin Laden" on *Frontline*, PBS, originally broadcast 1999, updated 2001, http://www.pbs.org/wgbh/pages/frontline/shows/binladen/etc/cron.html.

11. Peter BetBasoo, "Brief History of Assyrians," Assyrian International News Agency website, http://www.aina.org/brief.html.

12. "Assyrian of Armenia," People-in-Country-Profile, Joshua Project website,http:// www.joshuaproject.net/people-profile.php?peo3=10464&rog3=1Z.

13. BetBasoo, "Brief History."

14. Nineveh On Line, http://nineveh.com/whoarewe.htm.

15. Ibid.

16. BetBasoo, "Brief History."

17. This is using "Christian" in the world-religion sense of the word, i.e., Christendom.

18. Cahn, *Harbinger*, 53.

19. David T. Biggs, "Beyond the Towers: Performance of Masonry," Portland Cement Association website, http://www.cement.org/masonry/pp_fire_towers.asp.

20. Ibid.

21. Cahn, *Harbinger*, 61.

22. Jonathan Cahn, *The Isaiah 9:10 Judgment*, directed by George Escobar, (WND, 2012), DVD, 120 min. (Disc 1, at the 21:10 mark).

23. "Obama 'Fulfills' Isaiah 9:10 Prophecy – Again," WND.com, June 15, 2012, http:// www.wnd.com/2012/06/obama-fulfills-isaiah-910-prophecy-again/.

24. Cahn, *Harbinger*, 66.

25. Michael S. Heiser, PhD, "The Role of the Septuagint in the Transmission of the Scriptures," Associates for Biblical Research website, February 17, 2012, http://www.biblearchaeology.org/post/2012/02/17/The-Role-of-the-Septuagint-in-the-Transmission-of-the-Scriptures.aspx.

26. "New York granite is donated for Freedom Tower," Stone World website, August 4, 2004, http://stoneworld.com/articles/new-york-granite-is-donated-for-freedom-tower.

27. Dana Filipowski, "'Freedom Stone' to be Rededicated in Hauppauge at 9/11 Memorial Unveiling," LongIslandPress.com, August 13, 2009, http://www.longislandpress.com/2009/08/13/freedom-stone-to-be-rededicated-in-hauppauge-at-911-memorial-unveiling.

28. Cahn, *Harbinger*, 76.

29. Elmer B. Smick, "Gazit, 335" in *Theological Wordbook of the Old Testament*, edited by R. Laird Harris, Gleason L. Archer, Jr., and Bruce K. Waltke, electronic ed. (Chicago: Moody Press, 1999).

30. Exodus 20:25; 1 Kings 5:17, 6:36, 7:9, 11, 12; 1 Chronicles 22:2; Isaiah 9:10; Ezekiel 40:42; Lamentations 3:9; Amos 5:11.

31. Job 38:6; Psalm 118:2; Isaiah 19:13, 28:16; Jeremiah 51:26; Zechariah 10:4.

32. *New World Encyclopedia*, s.v. "Sycamore," http://www.newworldencyclopedia.org/entry/Sycamore.

33. "The Trinity Root," Trinity Wall Street website, http://www.trinitywallstreet.org/news/features/the-trinity-root.

34. Cahn, *Harbinger*, 90.

35. Ibid., Cahn citing *The Revell Bible Dictionary* (Grand Rapids: Fleming H. Revell, 1990), 198.

36. Cahn, *Harbinger*, 90.

37. AV, AV1873, KJV1900, NKJV, NASB, ESV, ASV, RSV, NRSV, NET, YLT, NIV, TNIV, Darby, HCSB, LEB, NCV, NLT, God's Word, Douay-Rheims.

38. Judges 9:15; 1 Kings 4:33, 5:6, 7:2; 2 Kings 14:9, 19:23; 2 Chronicles 2:8, 25:18; Ezra 3:7; Psalms 29:5, 92:12, 104:16; Song of Solomon 5:15; Isaiah 2:13, 14:8, 37:24; Jeremiah 22:23; Ezekiel 17:3, 27:5; 31:3, 31:8; Zechariah 11:1-2.

39. 2 Samuel 5:11, 7:2, 7:7; 1 Kings 5:8,10, 6:9,15,16,18,20,36, 7:3,7,11,12, 9:11; 1 Chronicles 14:1, 17:1, 22:4; 2 Chronicles 2:3; Isaiah 44:14; Jeremiah 22:14, 22:15.

40. Song of Solomon 1:17, 8:9; Amos 2:9.

41. Leviticus 14:4,6,49, 14:51,52.

42. Leviticus 19:6.

43. Isaiah 44:14.

44. "Plants of the Bible," Bartimaeus Alliance of the Blind, Inc. website, http://bartimaeus.us/pub_dom/plants_of_the_bible.html.

45. Numbers 24:6.

46. Job 40:17.

47. Psalm 80:10; Ezekiel 17:22,23.

48. *Common Trees of the Pacific Northwest*, s.v. "True Cedars (Cedrus)," Oregon State University website, http://oregonstate.edu/trees/conifer_genera/true_cedar.html.

49. 2 Samuel 6:5; Psalm 104:17; Song of Solomon 1:17; Ezekiel 27:5, 31:8.

50. 1 Kings 5:88; 2 Chronicles 2:8; Isaiah 14:8.

51. Isaiah 41:19, 44:14, 60:13.

52. Alternate translations are based on entries in *Theological Wordbook*, ed. Harris, et al, and James Strong, *Enhanced Strong's Lexicon*, (Bellingham, WA: Logos Bible Software, 2001).

53. Bible Plants, s.v. "Pines," Old Dominion University website, http://www.odu.edu/~lmusselm/plant/bible/aleppopine.php.

54. Taxonomy chart, https://www.msu.edu/~nixonjos/armadillo/taxonomy.html.

55. "Tree – Modern Taxonomy," http://science.jrank.org/pages/6943/Tree-Modern-taxonomy.html.

56. Taxonomy chart.

57. World Biomes, s.v. "Lebanon Cedar," http://www.blueplanetbiomes.org/lebanon_cedar.htm.

58. Neil Madison, "Norway Spruce (picea abies)," http://bioweb.uwlax.edu/bio203/s2009/madisen_neil/classification.html.

59. Cahn, *Harbinger*, 90-91.

60. Ibid., 92.

61. The Reverend Lyndon Harris, "Sanctuary at Ground Zero," National Geographic website, http://ngm.nationalgeographic.com/ngm/0209/st_pauls/online_extra.html.

62. The Reverend Lyndon Harris, quoted in "Rescue Work Was 'Spirit-Lifting,'" Trinity News, September 18, 2001, http://www.trinitywallstreet.org/news/articles/rescue-work-was-spirit-lifting-trinity-priest.

63. "Decorating Ground Zero's Tree of Hope," Trinity News, December 5, 2003, http://www.trinitywallstreet.org/news/articles/decorating-ground-zeros-tree-of-hope.

64. Roth, *Supernatural*, (at the 13:29 mark).

65. Cahn, *Harbinger*, 92.

66. Ibid., 104.

67. John Edwards, remarks to the Congressional Black Caucus Prayer Breakfast, September 11, 2004, http://www.presidency.ucsb.edu/ws/index.php?pid=84922#axzz1M02bgo9D.

68. Ibid.

69. Cahn, *Harbinger*, 108.

70. As counted using the search function of the Kindle for PC Reader.

71. Cahn, *Isaiah 9:10 Judgment*, (at the 44:38 mark).

72. Floor statement by Senate Majority Leader Tom Daschle, September 12, 2001, http://wfile.ait.org.tw/wf-archive/2001/010913/epf407.htm.

73. Cahn, *Harbinger*, 115.

74. Ibid., 117.

75. Ibid., 118.

CHAPTER 11

1. Cahn, *Harbinger*, 1.

2. Ibid., 129.

3. Ibid.

4. Ibid., 125.

5. Ibid., 127-28.

CHAPTER 12

1. This is also the title of chapter 15 of *The Harbinger*.

2. Cahn, Harbinger, 136.

3. Ibid., 73.

4. Ibid.

5. Ibid., 92.

6. Ibid., 94.

7. Ibid., 116.

8. Ibid., 136.

CHAPTER 13

1. Cahn, *Harbinger*, 136.

2. Ibid., 138.

3. The view that Isaiah 9:10 actually constitutes a vow is rather debatable. Although a declaration by Israel's leaders to the people, this does not necessarily make it a vow to God. However, given all the other problems in the book, this particular fine point is not necessarily worth debating.

4. Cahn, *Harbinger*, 139.

5. Ibid, 140.

6. Ibid.

7. Ibid., 142.

8. Ibid., 143.

9. Ibid., 142-43.

10. Ibid., 146.

11. Ibid., 147-48 (Non-essential parts of this dialogue have been omitted because of its length in the book. The breaks are indicated by "* * *" as line separators.).

12. Ibid., 149.

13. Ibid., 150-51.

14. Ibid., 151-52.

CHAPTER 14

1. Cahn, *Harbinger*, 159.

2. Ibid., 161.

3. Ibid., 159.

4. Ibid.

5. Ibid., 161.

6. Ibid., 159.

7. 1 Kings 17:1.

8. Ibid., 196.

9. "FHFA Conservator's Report – Why Fannie Mae And Freddie Mac Failed," Problem Bank List website, August 30, 2010, http://problembanklist.com/fhfa-conservators -report-why-fannie-mae-and-freddie-mac-failed-0183.

10. Cahn, *Harbinger*, 161.

11. "Case Study: The Collapse of Lehman Brothers," Investopedia website, April 2, 2009, http://www.investopedia.com/articles/economics/09/lehman-brothers-collapse .asp#axzz1sMPT0MMA.

12. Dr. John Rutledge, "Total Assets of the U.S. Economy $188 Trillion, 13.4xGDP," Rutledge Capital blog entry, May 24, 2009, http://rutledgecapital.com/2009/05/24 /total-assets-of-the-us-economy-188-trillion-134xgdp/.

13. "Did Lehman's Fall Matter?" from *Newsweek*, May 17, 2009, http://www.thedaily beast.com/newsweek/2009/05/17/did-lehman-s-fall-matter.html.

14. Cahn, *Harbinger*, 164.

15. Ibid., 164-65.

16. Ibid., 166.

17. Alexandra Twin, "Stocks Crushed," CNNMoney.com special report, September 29, 2008, http://money.cnn.com/2008/09/29/markets/markets_newyork/index.htm.

18. Harold Bierman, Jr., "The 1929 Stock Market Crash," Economic History Association website, February 5, 2010, http://eh.net/encyclopedia/article/bierman.crash.

19. Cahn, *Harbinger*, 163.

20. Ibid.

21. Ibid., 164.

22. Ibid., 170.

23. Ibid., 161.

24. Ibid.

25. Ibid., 165.

26. "Case Study: Collapse of Lehman."

27. Richard Simon and Nicole Gaouette, "Approval of bailout comes amid signs that a steep recession is just beginning," Los Angeles Times, October 4, 2008, http://articles.latimes.com/2008/oct/04/business/fi-bailout4.

28. Twin, "Stocks Crushed."

29. Ibid.

30. Ibid.

31. Alex Altman and Frances Romero, "Top 10 Dow Jones Drops," Time Specials, http://www.time.com/time/specials/packages/article/0,28804,1845523_1845619_1845553,00.html.

CHAPTER 15

1. Cahn, *Harbinger*, 195.

2. Ibid., 198.

3. Ibid., 206.

4. Ibid., 198.

5. Federal Hall information page, New York Architecture website, http://www.nyc-architecture.com/LM/LM050-FEDERALHALL.htm.

6. Home page, George Washington Masonic Memorial website, http://gwmemorial.org/

7. "A Brief History of the Memorial," George Washington Masonic Memorial website, http://gwmemorial.org/history.php

8. Phillip M. Thienel, "A Masonic Presence at Washington's Inauguration 200 Years Ago," Masonic World website, http://www.masonicworld.com/education/files/mar05/a_masonic_presence_at_washington.htm.

9. George Daniel MacGregor Pushee III, "Paul Revere – Grand Master," York Rite Freemasonry website, http://www.mwsite.org/papers/mwrevere.html.

10. "George Washington, The Mason," George Washington Masonic Memorial website, http://gwmemorial.org/washingtonTheMason.php.

11. Cahn, "Response from/In-Depth."

12. Cahn, *Harbinger*, 221-22.

CHAPTER 16

1. Genesis 6:5.

2. Cahn, *Harbinger*, 227-28.

3. Ibid., 229-30.

4. Ibid., 227.

5. Ibid., 233.

6. Ibid., 232.

7. Ibid., 235.

8. Ibid., 232.

9. Ibid., 231.

CHAPTER 17

1. Name Lab, Family Education website, http://genealogy.familyeducation.com/surname-origin/kaplan.

2. List of Jonathan Cahn's messages, Hope of the World website, http://www.hopeoftheworld.org/Order/index.php.

3. Judaism 101 website, s.v. "Kabbalah and Jewish Mysticism," http://www.jewfaq.org/kaballah.htm.

4. Kabbalah description, MileChai website, http://www.milechai.com/judaism/kabbalah.html.

5. Ibid.

6. Jonathan Cahn, "The Zohar Speaks," http://www.youtube.com/watch?v=RRzEnzsYqJs.

7. Judaism 101.

8. Cahn, "Zohar Speaks."

9. Ibid.

10. Ibid.

11. "5 Things You Should Know About The Zohar," Kabbalah website, http://www.kabbalah.info/engkab/mystzohar.htm.

12. Cahn, *Worldview Weekend*.

13. Jonathan Cahn, "Messiah's Cataclysm and The Hidden Writings of 30 A.D." http://www.youtube.com/watch?v=SFYwOP2cZzg.

14. Ibid.

15. Ibid.

CHAPTER 18

1. Cahn, *Harbinger*, 251.

2. 1 Corinthians 1:12.

3. Acts 17:10-11.

ABOUT THE BEREAN CALL

The Berean Call (TBC) is a non-denominational, tax-exempt organization which exists to:

ALERT believers in Christ to unbiblical teachings and practices impacting the church

EXHORT believers to give greater heed to biblical discernment and truth regarding teachings and practices being currently promoted in the church

SUPPLY believers with teaching, information, and materials which will encourage the love of God's truth, and assist in the development of biblical discernment

MOBILIZE believers in Christ to action in obedience to the scriptural command to "earnestly contend for the faith" (Jude 3)

IMPACT the church of Jesus Christ with the necessity for trusting the Scriptures as the only rule for faith, practice, and a life pleasing to God

A free monthly newsletter, THE BEREAN CALL, may be received by sending a request to: PO Box 7019, Bend, OR 97708; or by calling

1-800-937-6638

To register for free email updates, to access our digital archives, and to order a variety of additional resource materials online, visit us at:

www.thebereancall.org

 # ABOUT ABI

THE ALLIANCE FOR BIBLICAL INTEGRITY is an association of individual believers, churches, educational institutions, and organizations that are committed to the authoritative inerrant Word of God, an historical, grammatical interpretation of the Bible, and the historically accepted fundamentals of the faith. ABI seeks to equip believers to be faithful to the Lord and to His Word by teaching and promoting a biblical hermeneutic and worldview, while exposing and responding to unbiblical theology, practices, trends, and movements.

For more information, please visit ABI at:

www.biblicalintegrity.org